A DAMSEL IN DISTRESS

A Comedy of Youth, Love and Adventure in Three Acts

BY

IAN HAY

AND

P. G. WODEHOUSE

SAMUEL FRENCH, LTD.
26 SOUTHAMPTON STREET, STRAND, LONDON, W.C.2
59 CROSS STREET, MANCHESTER

SAMUEL FRENCH, INC.
25 WEST 45TH STREET, NEW YORK, U.S.A.
811 WEST 7TH STREET, LOS ANGELES, CAL.

SAMUEL FRENCH (CANADA), LTD.
480 UNIVERSITY AVENUE, TORONTO

FOR AMATEUR PRODUCTION ENQUIRIES

UNITED KINGDOM AND WORLD EXCLUDING NORTH AMERICA

plays@SamuelFrench-London.co.uk

020 7255 4302/01

Each title is subject to availability from Samuel French,

depending upon country of performance.

A DAMSEL IN DISTRESS

Produced at the New Theatre, London, on August the 12th, 1928, with the following cast :—

CHARACTERS

(In the order of their appearance.)

MAC (a Stage-door Keeper)	*Reginald Purdell.*
BILLIE DORE	*Isabel Wilford.*
GEORGE BEVAN	*Basil Foster.*
LADY MAUD MARSH	*Jane Baxter.*
PERCY, VISCOUNT TOTLEIGH	*Reginald Gardener.*
A POLICEMAN	*F. J. Arlton.*
ALBERT KEGGS	*Aubrey Mather.*
ALBERTINA KEGGS	*Clarice Hardwicke.*
LADY CAROLINE HIGGINS	*Helen Haye.*
THE EARL OF MARSHMORETON	*Clive Currie.*
ALICE FARADAY	*Celia Glynn.*
REGGIE HIGGINS	*Henry Kendall.*
DR. MOSSOP, DEAN OF DUMBLETON	*Philip Stanton.*
MRS. MOSSOP	*Vivienne Whitaker.*
LADY PRUDENCE WILLOWBY	*Ann Todd.*
CAPTAIN PLUMMER	*Guy Fletcher.*
MISS MOULD	*Joan Hickson.*
AUSTEN GRAY	*Thomas Weguelin.*

Tourists, ball-guests, footmen, postman, etc.

The play produced by NICHOLAS HANNEN.

SCENES

ACT I

ACT II

ACT III

To face page 5]

A DAMSEL IN DISTRESS

ACT I

SCENE 1.

The Interior of the Stage-door Entrance of the Regality Theatre. The stage-door itself is L., *opening on to the street.* R. *is an exit to the stage.* C. *is a half-door, opening into the stage-door keeper's box. The interior of the box is visible, with the usual clock, key-board, letter-rack, and telephone. The call-board and notice-board are outside,* R. *and* L. *of the box* C. *There is a wooden bench* R. *of the door.*

(As the CURTAIN *rises, in the street off* L. *a barrel-organ is playing cheerfully.* MAC, *the stage-door keeper, is inside his box, smoking and answering the telephone.*

Two chorus-girls enter from L. *They say* "Good morning, Mr. Mac," *and pass off* R. MAC *nods to them. A musician, with violin case, enters and goes off* R., *looking at the clock as he passes. The barrel-organ stops.* MAC *is now heard telephoning.)*

MAC (*gruffly*). Hullo! Yes, Regality Theatre, stage-door— that's us. Who do *you* want? Mr.——? No, he won't be here till after lunch to-day. (*Hanging up receiver.*)

(A POSTMAN *enters and deposits a bundle of letters on the ledge.)*

POSTMAN. Morning, Mac!

MAC. Morning! (*Taking letters.*) Quite a lot of waste paper this morning.

(*'Phone bell rings again.*)

Excuse me. (*Going to telephone again.*)

(*Exit* POSTMAN L.)

Hullo! Yes, it's Mac. Who? (*More genially.*) Oh, Mr. George Bevan. Good morning, sir. (*Listening.*) Yes, there's a full rehearsal at two-thirty—for cuts, I suppose. . . . Band rehearsal?

5

I've heard nothing about that, but there's a fiddler just came in. Kreisler, I think. Shall I ask him? You'll come over now? Very good, sir.

(*Sings song, hangs up receiver, and begins to distribute letters in pigeon-holes, humming. He examines some of the letters and chuckles over them. 'Phone bell rings again—*MAC *returns to the telephone, annoyed.*)

Hullo! Yes—Regality stage-door. Who? Flight Lieutenant——? How do you spell it? I can't put it down 'cause I've lost my indeliable pencil. All right. (*Listening.*) No, sir, I cannot give you her address—nor her telephone number, neither. Good morning. (*About to hang up—then.*) I suppose you know she's married, sir—and newly married? (*Hanging up, with a little nod of satisfaction.*)

(*Enter* L. BILLIE DORE, *a pretty young American actress of about 21— speaking to somebody outside stage-door* L. *of window.*)

BILLIE (*standing in doorway* L.). Good-bye, darling; it was marvellous of you to come. Oh, I say, don't forget Monday. All rightie. (*Entering and coming to door-keeper's box.*) Good morning, Mac!

MAC. Good morning, Miss Dore. There's a rehearsal at two-thirty sharp, for cuts.

BILLIE. Well, they can't hurt my part any.

MAC (*sympathetically*). Is it a long part?

BILLIE. I can just remember it, if I try hard. Any mail for me? (*Crossing and sitting on seat* R.)

MAC. I'll see, Miss. (*He takes letters out of the "D" pigeon-hole and thumbs them through.*)

(*The barrel-organ starts again, and is heard in the distance, faintly.*)

BILLIE. I guess that old boy will have some new tunes to play after this.

MAC. You mean after last night, Miss?

BILLIE. Yes. The Banana Girl's a big winner. That Hot Potato number went over big; and the Dutch Doll song, too. You've got to hand it to George Bevan as a melody-maker. That boy's whole score is a pippin. (*Lighting a cigarette.*) Did you see the show at all?

MAC. Me, Miss? No. I've been on the staff of this theatre for twenty-five years now, and—(*pointing* R.)—I don't think I've been through that door a dozen times.

BILLIE. Don't you ever get a night off?

MAC. Once in a blue moon. (*Taking up rest of the letters and examining them.*)

BILLIE. Well, what do you do with it?

MAC. I don't go to no theatre, Miss. I knows a better place.
But my old woman, she's a real theatre-goer, she is.

BILLIE. A regular first-nighter?

MAC. Yes; only she pays for her seat, of course. She was up
in our gallery last night, with the rest of the connossers.

BILLIE. What did they think up there?

MAC. 'Ighly satisfied, they were. They give us a year's run;
and they usually know.

BILLIE. They certainly do. That's great news for all of us.

MAC. For all of *you*, Miss. It makes no difference to me.
Triumph or disaster, wow or flop, I go on for ever—like one of them
permanent officials in the Foreign Office.

BILLIE. More like a permanent official in the Dead Letter Office.
Isn't there any mail for me at all?

(*Enter* GEORGE BEVAN, *a well-set-up young man of* 30.)

MAC. It's funny, I'm sure I saw your name somewhere. I'll
try the C's and E's, Miss. (*He does so.*)

(*The barrel organ stops.*)

GEORGE. Hallo, Billie!

BILLIE (*turning*). Why, look who's here. (*Meeting* GEORGE L.
of c. *door.*) If it isn't the king of jazz-merchants himself! Good
morning, George—and Little Billie's congratulations. (*Embracing
him.*)

GEORGE. Thank you, Billie; you're a dear. (*Moving to* R. *of*
c. *door.*) Good morning, Mac.

MAC. Good morning, Mr. Bevan. I've got a few telegrams for
you. (*Handing out a huge bundle.*)

GEORGE. Thank you.

BILLIE. Oh, look at the congratulations. Ain't it wonderful to
be popular?

GEORGE (*crossing to bench* R.). Not so wonderful. I shall have
to answer all these things. (*Sitting on* R. *of same.*) But don't you
get telegrams, Billie, like the rest of the profession?

BILLIE. I get letters mostly. The messages that those old men
out front send me couldn't be put into a telegram; somebody
might get arrested. I'll show you. Mac, have you found my mail
yet?

MAC (*handing out a bundle of letters*). Here you are, Miss. Unfor-
tunately I put 'em among the G's.

BILLIE. Thanks, Mac. (*Taking them, crossing to bench—and
sitting* L. *of* GEORGE.)

GEORGE. By the way, why weren't you at the party?

BILLIE. Was there a party?

GEORGE. There certainly was. I've been regretting the last
lobster cutlet ever since.

BILLIE. Was it a late show ?

GEORGE. We waited up for the morning papers.

BILLIE. Were the notices good ?

GEORGE. Fine.

BILLIE. They didn't say anything about my part, I suppose ? Two hips and one hooray !

GEORGE. Well—honestly—I don't quite re——

BILLIE. All right. I'll have to wait till next week for " The Era " as usual. They have a kind word for everybody. " Miss Billie Dore was also in the cast."

GEORGE. Still, why weren't you at the party ?

BILLIE. Me ? Because I was in bed. I hit the hay one hour after the curtain came down ! And I always do, when I can. I may be a Broadway Baby to look at, Georgie, and a hard-boiled little hoofer from the Great White Way, but I—(*rising and crossing to* L.)—was really intended to wear a sun-bonnet, and raise chickens, and be a village belle way back in the great open spaces.

GEORGE (*incredulously*). You *like* the country ?

BILLIE (*turning to* GEORGE). Like the country ? Me ? I wrote the words and music ! Do you know what I used to do when first I came over to this great burg of yours ? I used to walk around Covent Garden Market every morning sniffing the flowers and vegetables—kissing my hand to the roses, and saying " Hello, Cyril " to the brussels-sprouts. The big little hick, that's me !

GEORGE (*looking at her seriously*). Billie, I don't believe you.

BILLIE. I know you don't. And—(*showing letters*)—here's a bunch of saps who don't believe me either. (*Crossing and sitting* L. *of* GEORGE.) Mash notes, every one of them. Oh, boy, who would be a virtuous brunette ? Look at this one. (*Reading.*) " Dear little starry-eyed Stranger."

(GEORGE *groans, and snatches letter.*)

You appear to agree with me, George. Don't you ever get that way—fall for girls and send them mash notes ?

GEORGE. I never fell for a girl in my life. I've never been in love.

BILLIE (*rather annoyed*). Is that so ? And what's the matter with us ?

GEORGE. I'm living about five centuries after my time.

BILLIE. For heaven's sake ! Mac, listen to this ; it's going to be good. (*To* GEORGE.) All right, George, I'll ask you why. Why ?

(MAC *is washing his hands, and leans out of box listening as he dries his hands.*)

GEORGE. I ought to have been one of those romantic blighters who went about in armour on horseback, rescuing damsels in distress. Girls were girls then. They liked being rescued. They were very nice to people who rescued them. They swooned in their arms, and all that. Do you think if I rescued a girl to-day from being run over by a taxicab that she'd swoon in my arms? Not on your life. She'd kick me on the shins, and call me something that the taxi-driver would blush to hear. No, romance is dead. It's a flat, dull world. Nothing ever happens or ever will happen any more. (*Taking* Billie's *cigarette and smoking it.*)

Billie (*turning to* Mac, *indicating* George). And that is all brought about by one lobster cutlet too many.

Mac (*interposing from his box*). I don't think it's entirely that, Miss.

Billie. All right, Mac; now I'll ask you why. Why?

Mac. I think Mr. Bevan's blarzy, Miss. 'E's 'ad too much success—too much fat. That's what makes people blarzy. Besides, he's not married.

Billie. What difference does that make?

Mac. No married man ever thinks himself a success, Miss. His old woman sees to that.

(*Telephone bell rings, he goes to telephone.*)

Hullo! (*Listening.*) What? (*Listening again.*) You want two nice bundles of asparagus and a pair of bed-socks? (*Puzzled.*) Did you leave them under your seat last night, or something? (*Listening.*) Oh, you want to *order* them? (*Listening.*) No, madam, this is not Selfridge's. Good-by-ee. (*Hanging up receiver.*)

Billie (*picking out a letter*). Here's an invitation to lunch. I must beat it, George, and fix myself. (*Rising.*)

George. Oh, so you do accept invitations to lunch?

Billie. A poor girl must eat. But believe me, I'm a careful picker. (*Showing letter.*) This bird is mean, but safe. So long, George.

George. Have a good lunch!

Billie. I'll try.

George. Where is he taking you? Ciro's?

Billie. Ciro's? Don't make me laugh. That's where he takes me for pearls.

(*Exit* Billie.)

Mac. There's the orchestra tuning up, sir. Are you going to rehearse them?

George (*resignedly*). I suppose so—presently—with the accent on the hearse!

Mac (*glancing longingly at the clock*). Are you by any chance going to start for the next five minutes, sir? It's just gone half-past eleven, and they open quite prompt——

George. Carry on! I'll watch the door.

MAC. Thank you, sir. It's just a little matter of the one-thirty.

(*He hurries out* L.)

(GEORGE *continues to sit looking gloomily before him. Suddenly* LADY MAUD MARSH *rushes breathlessly in backwards and goes straight and hides in door-keeper's office. Slowly she peeps over the top and looks at* GEORGE, *who has just realized her presence. She is evidently much alarmed by something*—GEORGE'S *face breaks into a smile of incredulous astonishment and appreciation.*)

LADY MAUD. Good morning. (*Smiling.*)

GEORGE (*heartily*). Good morning. Isn't it a wonderful day? Sun shining and everything.

LADY MAUD. Good morning. Can I hide here, please?

GEORGE (*enthusiastically*). Of course you can hide. We'll both hide.

LADY MAUD. You're sure Percy won't see me here?

GEORGE. Percy? What an idea. No one shall ever see you again, except me. What's Percy's other name, by the way? And what's yours?

LADY MAUD. I can't tell you.

GEORGE. Oh, perhaps it will come back to you later. Mine's George Bevan.

LADY MAUD. Please watch Percy! (GEORGE *goes* L., *and looks off.*)

GEORGE. Is Percy something in white spats, with the general appearance of a blonde wart-hog at bay?

LADY MAUD. Yes; what is he doing now?

GEORGE. Apparently he's conducting a house-to-house search. He's just come up out of an area. Now he's peeping into a fried-fish shop. By Jove, he's crossing the street. He's coming in here. Get down on the floor, he shan't see you. (*He enters box and crouches down too out of sight.*)

(*Enter* PERCY, VISCOUNT TOTLEIGH. *He is a smallish, rather plump young man, dressed in the height of fashion, with white spats and top-hat. He has a receding chin and protruding eyes, and a stiff staccato manner. He raps on the floor with his stick.*)

PERCY. Porter!

GEORGE (*bobbing up from behind the door like a jack-in-the-box*). By your leave, sir?

PERCY (*starting back*). Here, I say!

GEORGE (*leaning on the door sill and blocking the view behind him*). Good morning, Percy.

PERCY. How the devil do you know my name's Percy?

GEORGE. It's written on that wall behind you.

(PERCY *of course turns round to look.* Immediately LADY MAUD'S *hand appears, plucking at* GEORGE'S *elbow. He looks down and smiles reassuringly.* PERCY *whirls round again.*)

PERCY. Don't talk damn nonsense, sir.

GEORGE. How are you going to understand me if I don't, Percy ?

PERCY. Don't call me Percy !

GEORGE. Very good, Douglas. Now what do you know this morning ?

PERCY. You're concealing a young lady.

GEORGE. Good gracious. Where ?

PERCY. How the devil do I know ? I'm searching for her. I'm going to look into that place behind you.

GEORGE. Why ?

PERCY. Because I'm sure she came in here. I've tried every other door in the street, and she's not there. So she must be here.

GEORGE (*admiringly*). The man of logic. (*Bowing and taking off his hat.*) Banzai ! But where is the man of action ? In other words, how are you going to get in here ? What about that, Osbert ?

PERCY (*advancing upon him threateningly*). Stand out of my way.

GEORGE. I won't.

PERCY (*thrusting his face close to* GEORGE'S). Then I'll force my way.

GEORGE. Cedric, you're blowing in my face. Good morning.

(*He picks off* PERCY'S *top-hat, pushes* PERCY *back, and throws the hat out of the stage-door.* PERCY *starts after it with a cry.*)

PERCY. That's a new hat.

(*After recovering hat, he returns and finds that* GEORGE *has stepped out of the box and is facing him.*)

GEORGE. Now will you get out ?

PERCY. I want my sister.

GEORGE (*interested*). Oh, she's your sister, is she ? I didn't know that.

PERCY (*triumphantly*). Then she is here ?

GEORGE (*blandly*). Who ?

PERCY (*shouting*). My sister, I want her ! I want my sister !

GEORGE. What you really want, old boy, is your nurse. Good-bye ! (*He tries to push* PERCY *out.*)

(PERCY *breaks away and makes a rush for the box.* GEORGE *seizes him, and they struggle fiercely. Finally* GEORGE *gets him as far as the door.* LADY MAUD'S *eyes appear above the sill, watching. There is increased noise in the doorway, and a third voice, evidently*

some one in the street joins in, inquiring " Now then, what's all
this ? "   " What's all this ? "   *A large* POLICEMAN *is now visible
in the doorway, mixed up with* GEORGE *and* PERCY.   GEORGE *gives*
PERCY *a sharp twist, and puts him into the arms of the* POLICEMAN,
then backs in towards the box again.   PERCY, *with his head down,
quite unconscious that he has changed opponents, punches the* POLICE-
MAN *vigorously.*)

PERCY.   You blackguard !   You infernal scoundrel !   I'll settle
you.
POLICEMAN (*solemnly*).   Now, now, now, *now* !   This won't do,
you know.

(PERCY *gives him another punch.*)

Here, stop it !   (*He gets* PERCY *by the collar and drags him o. with
one hand.   He is holding* PERCY'S *hat with the other.*)   What are
you two up to ?   You're committing a breach of the peace, you
know.   You can be charged for that.
PERCY (*getting his head up for a moment*).   Let me go !   Let me
go, I tell you.   It'll be the worse for you.
POLICEMAN (*pushing his head down again*).   Not so much of it !
GEORGE.   I'm so glad you arrived, officer.   I don't know who
this man is.   I was standing here five minutes ago, waiting for a
friend, when he rushed in and made a violent attack on me.   I'm
afraid he's been drinking.   A promising young fellow, too.
POLICEMAN.   Oh, so that's it !   (*To* PERCY.)   Now then, what
have you got to say ?
PERCY.   Take your filthy hands off me at once, damn you !
POLICEMAN (*incredulously*).   'Ullo !   'Ullo !   'Ullo !   Oh, oh, oh !
This won't do, you know.   It won't *do.*
PERCY (*suddenly wrenching himself free, screaming*).   You black-
guard.   How dare you ?

(PERCY *hurls himself at the* POLICEMAN *and butts him with his head.
The* POLICEMAN *closes with him, and after a brief struggle gets him
into the required position for being frog-marched out.*)

POLICEMAN.   That's done it.   A breach of the peace and assault-
ing a P.C.   You'll 'ave to come along with me now.
PERCY.   How dare you ?   Do you know who I am ?
POLICEMAN.   You can tell the Station Sergeant.   He'll want to
know.
PERCY (*getting his head up for a moment*).   I am Viscount Tot-
leigh, of Totleigh Castle, Totleigh, Hampshire.
POLICEMAN.   And I'm the Duke of Marlborough, of Marlborough
Police Palace, Great Marlborough Street, W.1, Middlesex.   Come
quietly.

(*He runs* PERCY *out.*)

(GEORGE, *overcome with laughter, watches them, then follows to the door. The moment his back is turned* LADY MAUD *slips out of the box and runs softly off* R.)

GEORGE. Good-bye, Percy. Give my love to the Duchess. (*Returning from the door rubbing his hands.*) God bless Sir Robert Peel. You can come out now. (*He sees the half-door standing open.*) 'Ullo! 'Ullo! 'Ullo! (*He finds the box empty—looks off* R., *much perplexed.*) What the—— (*He goes* R. *and gazes off, then makes a gesture of annoyance and starts back* C.)

(MAC *enters, wiping his mouth.*)

MAC. Was that a friend of yours I saw being took away sir?

GEORGE (*hurriedly*). Never mind him. Mac, is the front of the house open?

MAC. Yes, sir.

GEORGE. Then anybody going that way—(*pointing to* R.)—would get out by the front entrance?

MAC. Yes, sir.

GEORGE. Curses! (*Then he has an idea.*) Aha! Aha! Got an A B C?

MAC (*handing it out from his box*). Yes, sir. There you are.

GEORGE. That's the solution. Get me a taxi, will you, like a good chap? One with a driver under seventy, if possible. I'm pressed for time.

MAC. Yes, sir. (*He goes out and whistles.*)

(*Sound of a taxi approaching.*)

GEORGE (*turning over the leaves of* A B C). Totleigh Castle, Totleigh, Hampshire. (*Reading.*) Teddington, Toddington, Tony-pandy, Tooting, Totleigh—here we are. Totleigh. "Pop. 756. 83 miles."

MAC (*re-entering*). Your taxi, sir.

GEORGE. Thank you. (*Giving* MAC *a pound note.*) Put that on the two-thirty loser for me, will you?

MAC. Oh, thank you, sir, thank you! (*Following him to the door.*) Do you know anything, sir?

GEORGE. Yes, one thing—she lives at Totleigh, Hants! (*Shouting, outside.*) Waterloo!

(*The cab door is heard to bang and it starts off.*)

BLACK OUT.

SCENE 2.

The inner hall of Totleigh Castle, on a fine June morning. Tree-tops show above the low battlement wall outside the windows C., *indicating a steep drop.*

A door is up L., *and a massive fireplace is below, down* L. *Two chairs, one above and one below fireplace : a low-backed settee set up and down stage with back to fireplace. On the* R. *wall we have double doors, with lanterns on each side of them. The staircase above up* R., *leading up and off to* R. *A window on the stairs and a landing above. A high cane-backed settee is set* R.C., *facing to front, slightly on the oblique. A table is* L. *of windows* C. *and a stool* R. *of windows. Tapestries and pictures hang about the room and a suit of armour on stand up* R.C.

The EARL OF MARSHMORETON, *a short, sturdy, middle-aged man, in corduroys and a green baize apron, is pottering about outside the window, attending to his rose-trees.*

Enter L. ALBERT KEGGS, *the butler, a much more aristocratic figure than his master ; he resembles a retired bishop. He is followed by a* FOOTMAN *carrying a red rope, coiled up. The* FOOTMAN *hooks one end of the rope to a ring in the wall on the near side of the door.* KEGGS *takes the other and carries it solemnly to the other door, where he hooks it to another ring, on the far side, thus cutting off the staircase and window from the rest of the hall.*

Another FOOTMAN *enters, with two brass uprights, each about 3 feet high. These he sets out at intervals, to support the rope.*)

KEGGS (R.C., *regretfully*). Thursday seems to come round quicker than ever, 'Enery.

FIRST FOOTMAN (L.C.). Yes, Mr. Keggs.

KEGGS. And this 'ot weather seems to bring the proletariat out like insects. Two charabancs this morning, I hear—and another girls' school. Draw the rope tight, Thomas.

SECOND FOOTMAN (L.). Yes, Mr. Keggs.

KEGGS. Last Thursday a couple of young 'uzzies actually climbed over it, and sat on that fender, as bold as brass.

SECOND FOOTMAN (*respectfully*). Tut-tut-tut! (*Moving to door* L.)

KEGGS. I don't know what the middle classes are coming to, these days. (*Examining one of the uprights.*) Where's that girl Albertina ?

SECOND FOOTMAN. In the outer 'all, Mr. Keggs, doing a bit of polishing.

KEGGS. Then direct her to come and do a bit of it in here.

SECOND FOOTMAN. Yes, Mr. Keggs.

(*Exit door* L.)

To face page 14]

KEGGS (*putting up printed notices :* "Kindly keep in line" *and* "Kindly do not finger objects of art* "). Why people should want to pay a shilling a head to be led round like dumb animals, gaping at the interiors of their betters, is a thing I never could understand. It only makes them feel envious of us.

(*During this* ALBERTINA KEGGS *has appeared from the door* L. *She is a pert young between-maid. She carries a polishing cloth.*)

ALBERTINA. Still, the shillings come in useful, Mr. Keggs.

KEGGS (*starting slightly, but maintaining his dignity*). That is true, Albertina. They go to a deserving charity.

ALBERTINA (*gently*). Yes, Mr. Keggs—a charity what begins at home.

KEGGS (*sharply*). What do you imply by that ?

ALBERTINA. You 'ave got a 'ome, 'aven't you, Mr. Keggs ?

(HENRY, *the* FIRST FOOTMAN, *sniggers.*)

KEGGS. That'll be all, Henry !

HENRY (*his laugh fading away*). Yes, Mr. Keggs.

(*Exit door* L.)

KEGGS (*approaching threateningly*). Now, my girl, get to work on that brass ; and put some elbow-grease into it.

ALBERTINA (*kneeling and getting to work, polishing the brass stand*). Yes, Uncle Albert. (L.C.)

KEGGS. And tell me what you meant by that allusion to charity.

ALBERTINA. I was only admiring the 'ead you've got for figures—that's all.

KEGGS (*glaring*). What are you 'arping on, my girl ?

ALBERTINA. You know. That sweepstake.

KEGGS. Not so loud ! (*Looking quickly to* R. *and* L.) What about it ?

(ALBERTINA *produces a slip of paper and hands it to him.*)

ALBERTINA. What does that say ?

KEGGS. It says "Mr. X." It's all in order. It means you've drawn The Field.

ALBERTINA. It is a funny thing, whenever we get up a sweepstake about anything, you draw the favourite and I draw the field.

KEGGS. My girl, I treat your insinuation with contempt.

ALBERTINA. Do you ? Well, here's another funny thing about this sweepstake. We drew it six months ago, and nothing 'as 'appened since. When does the balloon go up ? When do we touch ?

KEGGS. Sometimes I feel sorry my poor brother Sam ever had a daughter.

ALBERTINA (*firmly*). Tell me, or I blab.

KEGGS (*softly*). You little viper.

ALBERTINA (*imitating him*). You big stiff ! Tell me !

KEGGS (*climbing down*). Well it's this way. We think—the upper servants that is—that Lady Maud will make up her mind to get married any day now. The old girl has been seeing to that. That's why there's to be this ball.

ALBERTINA. I suppose she wants to get Maud's mind off that chap she met in Switzerland a year ago.

KEGGS. What do you know about it ?

ALBERTINA. I can get my head nearer to a keyhole than what you can; it's not so fat. Carry on, Uncle.

KEGGS (*after giving her a venomous look*). Well, the ball ought to bring things to a head. All the eligible gentlemen in the county are coming, and we 'ave a feeling that Maud's engagement to one of 'em will be settled that very evening. 'Ence the sweepstake. Of course the favourite is young Reggie.

ALBERTINA. Yes, and you drew him ! (*Rubbing at brass.*)

KEGGS. I was so fortunate.

ALBERTINA. And I was not. Who is " Mr. X " ?

KEGGS. He's the dark horse. If her young ladyship turns down Mr. Reggie and all the county gentlemen and marries some total stranger, that's Mr. X, and you win the sweepstake.

ALBERTINA (*rising*). And then I suppose that you'll find there's been a mistake in the draw, and " Mr. X " really belongs to you ?

KEGGS. 'Ush !

LADY CAROLINE (*is heard speaking off up* R.). All right, Miss Faraday ; I'll send for you when I want you.

(ALBERTINA *rubs briskly—*KEGGS *arranges furniture.*)

(LADY CAROLINE HIGGINS, *carrying housekeeping book, appears on the stairs. She is a stately lady of about* 45.)

LADY CAROLINE (*noticing the rope*). Oh dear, is this Thursday ?

KEGGS. I fear so, my lady.

LADY CAROLINE (*crossing to* C.). Open all the doors and windows after they have gone, Keggs.

KEGGS. Yes, my lady.

LADY CAROLINE (*moving up* L.C.). Has a telephone message arrived from Master Percy ?

KEGGS. No, my lady.

LADY CAROLINE. It's most upsetting. I can't think where he can be. So unlike him to stay away all night. He never enjoys strange beds. Mr. Reggie, too. Why did he go up to town yesterday ? (*Putting book on table* L. *of windows.*)

KEGGS. I couldn't say, my lady. He went off in his car after breakfast, without advising me.

(There is a sudden uproar outside the window o.*)*

LORD MARSHMORETON (*off*). Confound that bucket !
LADY CAROLINE. Good gracious—what's that ?
KEGGS. His lordship, my lady.

(Enter by the window LORD MARSHMORETON, *carrying a rose-bush
in a tub. He is addressing the rose-bush.*)

LORD MARSHMORETON. Of all the damned, infernal, god-forsaken
little pests——
LADY CAROLINE (*crossing to* R.). Harry ! Keggs, take your
niece away.

*(*KEGGS *goes out by the door* L., *holding* ALBERTINA *firmly by the
arm.*)

Harry, what *is* the matter ?
LORD MARSHMORETON (*furiously*). Matter ? Look at that.
See them ! Crawling, seething—multiplying under my very nose,
damn it ! Curse them—every single million of them. Look !
(He thrusts the bush under LADY CAROLINE'S *nose.*)
LADY CAROLINE (*starting back*). What are they ?
LORD MARSHMORETON. What are they ? You've been my
sister for forty-five years—me, the best known rose-grower in the
South of England—and you ask me what these are ? They're
thrips—aphides—parasites—green-fly—devils ! (*Passing* LADY
CAROLINE, *who retreats down* R.) Where's that whale oil ? I'll
show them who's master in this house. (*Putting down rose-bush* o.
and going out by window, returning with bucket and syringe.)
LADY CAROLINE (*sitting on settee by stairs*). Harry, restrain yourself ! I want to talk to you.
LORD MARSHMORETON (*examining leaves of the bush*). What is
it ?
LADY CAROLINE. Where is Reggie ?
LORD MARSHMORETON. I don't know. He's your son—not
mine, thank God ! (*Bending over rose.*)
LADY CAROLINE. Then where's Percy ? He's your son.
LORD MARSHMORETON. Yes, damn it ! What do you want him
for ?
LADY CAROLINE. To discuss his coming-of-age festivities, less
than a week away. A hundred things to see to, and Percy must
choose this moment to sleep in town. Why can't people stay in
their homes, I wonder ?
LORD MARSHMORETON. You went away yourself a couple of
nights ago.
LADY CAROLINE. For twenty-four hours—on imperative public
business——
LORD MARSHMORETON. Where ?

B

LADY CAROLINE. To address the girls at the Southern Counties. Orphanage.

LORD MARSHMORETON. Wretched little devils! (*Squirts vigorously.*)

LADY CAROLINE. What?

LORD MARSHMORETON (*indicating the rose-bush*). These things! Go on.

LADY CAROLINE. And when I come back, what do I find? An empty house. Percy away—Reggie away——

LORD MARSHMORETON (*sharply*). Was Maud away?

LADY CAROLINE. No, Maud was here.

(LADY MAUD *appears on the staircase.*)

LORD MARSHMORETON. Where is she now?

LADY MAUD. Here I am, Daddy. Good morning, darling. (*She runs across and jumps into her father's arms.*)

LORD MARSHMORETON. God bless my soul! Hold hard!

(*They embrace affectionately.*)

LADY MAUD (*turning to* R.). Good morning, Aunt Caroline.

(LORD MARSHMORETON *kneels by rose-bush.*)

LADY CAROLINE (*rising*). Good morning, dear. Have you checked that list of acceptances for the ball? The caterer must have it to-day.

LADY MAUD (*hesitating*). Not quite—yet—Auntie.

LADY CAROLINE. But I left everything ready for you to begin before I went away.

LADY MAUD. Well, you see, yesterday morning was so lovely that I thought I would spend it—out of doors.

LADY CAROLINE (*meaningly*). Did you go far?

LADY MAUD. Oh no—not very far.

LADY CAROLINE. You haven't forgotten your father's orders, I hope, about London being out of bounds?

LADY MAUD. Oh no, Auntie.

LORD MARSHMORETON (*still kneeling by rose*). You haven't been seeing that infernal fellow again, have you? That half-starved poet you met in Switzerland? Hey?

LADY MAUD. I haven't set eyes on him for over a year.

LORD MARSHMORETON. Good girl!

LADY MAUD. What chance have I had? Watched all the time!

LORD MARSHMORETON. But you've forgotten all about him now —hey?

LADY MAUD (*with spirit*). No, I haven't—and never will. So there.

(LORD MARSHMORETON *gives a despairing glance at his sister—then makes a sudden onslaught on the rose-bush with the syringe.*)

LORD MARSHMORETON.   Gurr!   Drink that!   I'll teach you to harbour thrips.

LADY CAROLINE.   Harry—look at the mess.   Whale oil all over the carpet.   Maud, ring for Keggs.

(MAUD *takes a running jump over the rope, then rings the bell by fireplace.*)

Maud, don't do that.

LADY MAUD.   Sorry, Auntie, but I get so little exercise these days.   (*She unfastens the rope at the L. end and walks back demurely, leaving the rope unfastened.*)

(*Enter* KEGGS *with newspapers from L.*)

LADY CAROLINE.   Keggs, send some one to clean up this mess.

KEGGS.   Very good, my lady.   Here are the morning papers. (*Laying them on table up L. of windows, then exits door L., looking at mess on floor with pained expression.*)   Tut-tut!

LADY CAROLINE (*sitting on settee R.*).   Maud dear, run upstairs and tell Miss Faraday to come here.

LADY MAUD.   Yes, Auntie.   (*Goes upstairs.*)

(*On hearing* MISS FARADAY'S *name* LORD MARSHMORETON *collects his rose-bush, etc., and sets off stealthily towards the window—* LADY CAROLINE *calls after him.*)

LADY CAROLINE.   Harry, don't go away!

LORD MARSHMORETON (*defiantly*).   Why not?

LADY CAROLINE.   Miss Faraday is coming down.   This is a good opportunity for you and her to have a nice long day with the Family History.   It's quite time you finished off that seventy-second chapter.

LORD MARSHMORETON.   I won't!

LADY CAROLINE.   And I want to speak to you about Maud. She and Reggie must come to an understanding at once.   She's more than half in love with him already; they've known each other from childhood; and with their combination of brains and beauty——

LORD MARSHMORETON.   Which of the two does Reggie represent?

LADY CAROLINE.   What a question!   Of course he's handsome as well——

LORD MARSHMORETON (*resignedly*).   All right.   You win.   (*Putting down plant again and sitting beside* LADY CAROLINE.)   But what about this slimy poet she's being so romantic about—hey?

LADY CAROLINE.   Maud was only a child last year.   When she has been married to Reggie for six months, she'll be insensible to everything else.

LORD MARSHMORETON. So far as my observation goes, Reggie's insensible most of the time himself, so they'll be a pair. But I don't believe in Reggie for Maud, all the same. What's this other fellow like? What's his infernal name?

LADY CAROLINE. I don't know; Maud wouldn't tell me. I'm afraid she still corresponds with him. She's as obstinate as you, Harry.

LORD MARSHMORETON. I'm not obstinate. (*Emphatically.*)

LADY CAROLINE. Hush!

(*Enter* MISS FARADAY *down the staircase with books and ledgers. She is a demure, pretty girl of about* 23.)

MISS FARADAY. You sent for me, Lord Marshmoreton?

LORD MARSHMORETON. No. (*Trying to rise.*)

LADY CAROLINE (*pushing him down again*). Yes! His lordship is anxious to get on with the Family History this morning, Miss Faraday.

LORD MARSHMORETON (*rising and backing towards the windows* C.). No, I'm not! (*Picking up tub of roses.*)

LADY CAROLINE. Harry, don't be childish! Go upstairs and change. You look like a jobbing gardener. (*Pause.*) Be ready in twenty minutes, Miss Faraday.

MISS FARADAY. Certainly. (*Crossing* L. *to* LORD MARSHMORETON.) I have the notes prepared for the story of Leonard's Leap.

(LADY CAROLINE *takes up a newspaper and glances through it.*)

LORD MARSHMORETON (*on stairs, blazing out*). Oh, curse Leonard —and his Leap! Curse everything! Am I never to have any peace? One of these days I shall pack a carpet-bag and walk right out of this place, and you'll never see me again. And then will you be sorry? (*Shouting.*) No!

LADY CAROLINE (*with a startled cry*). Heavens above! Harry, read that. Now we know where Percy slept last night. (*Showing paper.*) Look! "Peer's son in a Theatrical Brawl." "Viscount Totleigh charged at Marlborough Street."

LORD MARSHMORETON (*leaning over staircase and snatching paper*). Assaulting a policeman. "The officer complained that the accused lowered his head and butted him savagely in the pit of the stomach." (*Delightedly.*) Oh, well done, Percy! (*Coming down the stairs to settee.*)

LADY CAROLINE. Harry, your own son! (*Snatching the paper from him.*)

LORD MARSHMORETON. I didn't think he had it in him. I'm very pleased about this. Does it say what they gave him?

LADY CAROLINE. No,—(*reading*)—he comes up this morning.

LORD MARSHMORETON. Well, I'll pay the damage, whatever it is. (L. *of settee.*)

LADY CAROLINE (*frantically*). Suppose they put him in gaol for a month ? (*Rising and crossing frantically up to window and down again.*)

LORD MARSHMORETON. Then we can call off the ball ! Splendid. (*Who is between the ladies, struck by a thought.*) I suppose it *was* Percy. It sounds much more like Reggie—(*to* MISS FARADAY) doesn't it ? He would butt a policeman in the stomach for twopence.

MISS FARADAY (*unguardedly*). I don't think so at all, Lord Marshmoreton. Mr. Reggie is very unfairly judged by some people. All he needs is a little kindly guidance. (*Crossing to* R. *and making her exit upstairs.*)

(LORD MARSHMORETON *and* LADY CAROLINE *stare incredulously after* MISS FARADAY.)

LADY CAROLINE. There seems to be some confusion in that young woman's mind as to whether I am Reggie's mother or she is.

LORD MARSHMORETON. I'll go and telephone to Marlborough Street. Not that I have much hope. Such news about Percy seems too good to be true.

(*Crossing to* L. *and bumping into* ALBERTINA—*with bucket, who has just entered.*)

Oh confound you !

(*To* KEGGS, *who has entered, following* ALBERTINA. *Holding the door open for his lordship, who exits.*)

KEGGS (*coming to* C. *after closing the door—to* ALBERTINA). That's the place, my girl. Mop it up.

(ALBERTINA *sets to work*—KEGGS *approaches* LADY CAROLINE *at the settee* R.C.)

My lady, might I speak to you ? It's about Master Percy's festivities.

LADY CAROLINE (*rising*). Festivities ? Really, Keggs—— (*Indignantly facing to* R.)

KEGGS. I was referring to the approaching festivities, my lady, in connection with Lord Totleigh's majority.

LADY CAROLINE. Oh ! (*Turning.*)

KEGGS. The ball. Are additional waiters being sent down from town by the caterer, or am I to make myself responsible for engaging local talent ?

LADY CAROLINE (*distractedly*). I don't even know if Master Percy will be here for the ball. He may be somewhere else entirely different. Oh, why don't we hear from him ? This silence is unbearable.

(*There is a prolonged screech from a motor-horn outside, repeated several times.*)

Whose car is that?

KEGGS. Mr. Reggie's, my lady, most decidedly.

LADY CAROLINE. Well, go and let him in.

(KEGGS *hurries out by the door* L.—LADY CAROLINE *goes out by the window and looks frantically down over the battlements.* LORD MARSHMORETON *reappears from door* L.)

Reggie is here. He may know something.

LORD MARSHMORETON. It will be for the first time in his life if he does.

(*Noticing* ALBERTINA, *who is listening.*)

Tell that little reptile to go away.

LADY CAROLINE. Reptile? Where? Oh, you can go, Albertina.

ALBERTINA. Yes, my lady. (*She approaches the door* L.)

(*Simultaneously the door is thrown open and* REGGIE HIGGINS *appears. He is a tall young man with a genial manner and a limited vocabulary —a " nut " of the first water. He is wearing a motor-coat and goggles—these he removes as he enters.*)

REGGIE (*with a friendly smile to* ALBERTINA). Hallo, Albertina. Toodle-oo!

ALBERTINA (*politely*). Pip, pip, sir.

(*Exit reluctantly by door* L.)

LADY CAROLINE (*running to him*). Reggie, my boy.

REGGIE. What-ho, Mum!

(*They embrace.* LADY CAROLINE *helps him off with coat and hat.*)

What-ho, Uncle Harry! Do we hold the post-mortem in here?

LADY CAROLINE. What do you mean, Reggie?

REGGIE. Mean? I mean Percy. I've got his body outside.

LORD MARSHMORETON. Is he dead, damn it?

REGGIE. Dead? Oh no. Oh dear no! A bit shop-soiled, but good for several seasons yet. He's in the outer hall, with Keggs, hanging back in the collar a bit. (*Chuckling.*) Not that he *has* a collar, but——

LADY CAROLINE (*frantically*). Tell me the worst. Why doesn't he come in?

REGGIE. Well, he's not quite sure of his reception. Have you seen the morning papers?

LADY CAROLINE. Yes.

REGGIE. Very well, then. Percy the Policeman Puncher.

Percy the Prodigal. (*To* LORD MARSHMORETON.) Which is it to be, sir—the Fatted Calf or the Royal Raspberry ?

LORD MARSHMORETON. Why, it's the best thing he's ever done in his life !

REGGIE. The Fatted Calf. All is forgiven. (*Crossing* L. *to the door.*) Come along in, Percy, out of the snow. The old folks are watching and waiting in the parlour.

(*Enter* PERCY, *holding* KEGGS'S *arm. He helps* PERCY *to the settee* L.C., *where* PERCY *sits down. His clothes are dishevelled, one of his spats is gone, and he has no collar or tie.* LORD MARSH- MORETON *and* LADY CAROLINE *stand gazing at him, transfixed. A footman enters, hands whisky-and-soda to* PERCY *and goes out.* ALBERTINA *is seen outside the door peeping in.* KEGGS *takes her by the neck and leads her away.*)

(*Proudly.*) Look him over once or twice. Percy, the Human Tiger.

LADY CAROLINE. Percy, how did it all happen ?

LORD MARSHMORETON. What the devil came over you ? You've never done anything in your life before but collect prayer-mats and old china, and wear flannel next to your skin. What happened ? Did you get sunstroke, or something ?

(PERCY *gives* LADY CAROLINE *a look of indescribable suffering, then takes a deep drink.*)

REGGIE. He's been like that all the way down from town. The Silent Tomb was chatty by comparison.

LADY CAROLINE (*crossing and sitting by* PERCY). Percy, I implore you. You are my favourite nephew—the only member of this family who has kept, so far, out of the Sunday papers. There must be an explanation. Tell us !

PERCY (*clearing his throat and beginning in a weak voice*). I was walking along Piccadilly yesterday morning, on my way to my tailor's——

(REGGIE *has gone* C. *and joined* LORD MARSHMORETON. *They turn and chuckle to one another.*)

LORD MARSHMORETON (*looking at* PERCY'S *clothes*). You don't seem to have got there, my boy.

LADY CAROLINE (*turning to them*). Hush !

PERCY. When suddenly, just outside Fortnum and Mason's, I saw Maud.

LADY CAROLINE. Maud ? But Maud was here yesterday.

REGGIE. Of course she was.

PERCY. No, she wasn't. She was in Piccadilly. I wasn't sure if it was her at first, so I followed her.

REGGIE (to LORD MARSHMORETON). Percy the Pursuer.

PERCY (after glaring at REGGIE). Suddenly she turned round and saw me, and began to hurry. Then I was sure. I chased her through Piccadilly Circus——

REGGIE. Did you go straight across, or did you conform to the merry-go-round ?

LADY CAROLINE. Don't interrupt him, Reggie.

PERCY. She went up Shaftesbury Avenue—practically running now—with me close behind. Suddenly she turned up a little side street. When I got round the corner she was gone. I knew she must be hiding somewhere quite close, so I tried all the openings. Finally I came to the stage-door of a theatre. That didn't stop me. I forced my way in ; and there she was, in a hutch—with a man.

REGGIE. You mean with a rabbit.

PERCY (angrily). No ! With a man. The man, of course.

LADY CAROLINE. But what was she doing in a hutch, darling ?

PERCY. I mean a sort of cage, where stage-door keepers live. She must have been sitting on the floor inside ; I think I saw the top of her head. The man was inside too, trying to block the view.

LADY CAROLINE. What did you do then ?

PERCY. I told the fellow, quite civilly, that I wanted my sister. He made an insulting reply, and finally tipped my hat off.

(REGGIE and LORD MARSHMORETON both guffaw—then check themselves.)

After that, of course, I chastised him.

LADY CAROLINE. Did you hurt him much, dear ?

PERCY. Well, naturally, I had to give him a lesson. I had just knocked him down for the third time, when a most officious policeman came in and tried to interfere. So I knocked him down too.

LADY CAROLINE. Right down ?

PERCY. Well, I gave him a good punishing blow.

LADY CAROLINE. Where ?

LORD MARSHMORETON. He butted him in the pit of the stomach.

LADY CAROLINE. Hush.

REGGIE. Percy, the humane killer.

PERCY (having finished his drink). Of course it was an injudicious thing to do, but one sees red on these occasions. After that he arrested me and took me to Marlborough Street. I told them who I was, and they telephoned to Reggie for me ; but he was out at a party, and only turned up this morning.

LADY CAROLINE (in a horrified voice). And you spent the night in Marlborough Street ?

PERCY. Yes, I did.

LORD MARSHMORETON. They always used to take me to Vine Street. A better class of place altogether.

LADY CAROLINE. And what did they do to you in the morning, dear?

REGGIE (*cheerfully*). Five pounds and costs.

LADY CAROLINE. But what happened to Maud and the man?

PERCY. I don't know. I suppose they got away in the confusion. I was quite as much as one policeman could tackle.

LADY CAROLINE. And you are sure it was *the* man—the poet from Switzerland?

PERCY. Oh, undoubtedly. He called me Percy. Maud must have told him all about me.

LADY CAROLINE. What was he like?

PERCY. A horrible-looking fellow.

(LADY MAUD *appears on the staircase with golf clubs. She does not notice anything unusual at first.*)

(LADY CAROLINE *rises.*)

LADY MAUD. Hallo, Reggie! Back home, then? Come and have nine holes on the garden course before lunch.

REGGIE. Right-ho! Right-completely-ho! I'll carry your clubs, Maud. (*Going to her quickly and whispering.*) I've told them nothing.

LADY CAROLINE (*who has risen and is standing in front of* PERCY). Maud! (*Stepping aside.*) Look at your handiwork.

(LADY MAUD *sees* PERCY *for the first time—she gives a faint scream, and gazes at him round-eyed. Then she catches* REGGIE'S *eye and bursts into helpless laughter; so does* REGGIE; *so does* LORD MARSHMORETON.)

Maud! Is this the time for hilarity? I wish to ask you some questions. Where were you yesterday morning?

LADY MAUD (*coming c. and standing behind the rope, grasping it like a prisoner in the dock*). In bed.

(REGGIE *stands beside her.*)

LADY CAROLINE. In bed?

LADY MAUD. Yes, at first. Of course I got up for breakfast.

REGGIE. Two boiled eggs and a slice of ham. I cut it for her myself. The alibi is complete.

LADY CAROLINE. Where were you for the rest of the day?

LADY MAUD. I went out for a bit.

LADY CAROLINE. Where?

LADY MAUD. Oh, the garden—the stables—the garage——

LORD MARSHMORETON (*coming down, interposing*). What were you doing at eleven o'clock in a hutch? Hey?

LADY MAUD. A hutch?

LADY CAROLINE. Maud, did you or did you not go to London yesterday?

(LORD MARSHMORETON *turns and goes up stage.*)

LADY MAUD (*boldly*). Yes.

LADY CAROLINE. How did you get there?

LADY MAUD. By car.

LADY CAROLINE. Did you drive yourself?

LADY MAUD. No.

LADY CAROLINE. Who did?

REGGIE. I did.

LADY CAROLINE. You?

REGGIE. Yes. " I, he said gently, in my little Bentley." Goodbye, everybody. (*Turning to go.*)

LADY MAUD. Coward!

REGGIE. All right. I'll stay.

LADY CAROLINE. And you went to London to meet that man?

LADY MAUD. Yes, I did.

LADY CAROLINE. After having been forbidden to see him again?

LADY MAUD. Well, I di—— (*Checking herself—and turning to* LADY CAROLINE. *Releasing rope with left hand.*) You can't stop yourself from caring for somebody, Auntie.

LADY CAROLINE (*to* LORD MARSHMORETON). Harry, say something to her.

LORD MARSHMORETON (*to* LADY MAUD). Not stop yourself from——? Oh yes, you can. I remember being desperately in love with a girl once—at Oxford—(*coming down*)—in a tea shop. I used to hold her hand across a damned cold marble table for hours. I wanted to marry her; so my old dad took me away and practically locked me up here until she married a milkman. I thought I should never get over it. Let me see—what was her name? Gladys, Rosie, Charlotte—damme, I've forgotten it!

LADY CAROLINE. But that's just it. You'll forget too, Maud, when you've been locked up a little——

LADY MAUD. Locked up?

LADY CAROLINE. Yes, as your father suggests. You will not go outside the lodge gates till further notice.

LADY MAUD. Stone walls do not a prison make, nor——

LADY CAROLINE. No, but they make a very good imitation, dear. Then that's settled. (*Rising.*) Percy, go upstairs and change those trousers.

PERCY. Oh, dear! (*Going slowly upstairs, glaring back at* REGGIE *and* LADY MAUD, *who stand arm-in-arm watching him.*)

LADY CAROLINE. And, Percy, have a bath.

PERCY. Must I? They washed me twice at Marlborough Street.

LORD MARSHMORETON (*looking after him as he disappears*). Five
pounds and costs. I'll pay it myself.
LADY CAROLINE. Harry, Miss Faraday will be here any moment.

(REGGIE *becomes much agitated.*)

LORD MARSHMORETON. Do you think I'm going to bother with
a mouldy history to-day ?   My son at Marlborough Street for butting
a policeman in the stomach. It's a gala day.

(*Exit by window with rose-bush.*)

LADY CAROLINE (*going to* LADY MAUD *and* REGGIE). Maud,
darling, I don't want to be unkind, but you must stay in the grounds
until this silly infatuation is over. I'm sure Reggie will be glad
to help you to pass the time. (*To* REGGIE.) Won't you, dear ?
REGGIE. Rather !
LADY CAROLINE. I knew you would. (*To* LADY MAUD.) I
was glad to notice that you turned to Reggie for help even in that
foolish escapade of yesterday. Now I must run off. (*Goes* R.)
You will soon learn who your true friends are, Maud.

(*Exits upstairs.*)

(*Pause.* REGGIE *and* LADY MAUD *turn and regard one another.*)

REGGIE. Oho !
LADY MAUD. Aha ! (*Moving slightly to* L. *and turning to speak.*)
REGGIE. She's still at the old game. Always trying to contract
alliances. (*Crossing* LADY MAUD.)
LADY MAUD. And it's all so superfluous, isn't it ?
REGGIE. Absolutely. (*Pause.*) Dear Maud !

(REGGIE *and* LADY MAUD *go right up to each other.*)

LADY MAUD. Darling Reggie. You won't marry me, will you ?
REGGIE (*heartily*). Not at any price, my precious.
LADY MAUD. Oh, bless you ! (*Embracing him warmly.*)
REGGIE. The fact is, I am utterly and hopelessly pots about
somebody else.

(*Continue embracing with heads side by side.*)

LADY MAUD. That's wonderful.
REGGIE. Not too wonderful. Maud, how does love take you ?
LADY MAUD. It makes me all dreamy, and rather happy, and
rather miserable—and I want to read poetry all day.
REGGIE. But in the actual presence of the adored one. How
do you comport yourself ?
LADY MAUD. I just sit, and look, and listen.
REGGIE. Yes, I do that too ; but chiefly because I have to.

(*Finish embrace.*)

Have you ever suffered from elephantiasis of the hands and feet ?

LADY MAUD. I don't think so.

REGGIE. Well, that's what I get in the presence. The limbs swell; I can't move them. I can't think. I can't speak. The tongue becomes dry and furry; the forehead glistens. That sort of thing gives the girl the wrong idea about you; it makes her think you are a chump. What is one to do in the circumstances ? (*Sitting on the settee* L.C. *by fire.*)

LADY MAUD (*smiling*). Put your arm round her waist, and tell her you love her.

REGGIE. But I can't.

LADY MAUD. Why ?

REGGIE. Because I never have time. You can't go straight up to a girl and put your arm round her waist and say " I love you." She'd send for the police if you did. You have to lead up to it. A few general topics to start with. Politics. The crops. Sport; the two-thirty winner. Then, winners in general. Then you say you would like to be a winner yourself some day. Winner of a matchless prize. And so forth. You get the idea ?

(LADY MAUD *nods.*)

But just as you get so far, and the arm is starting out on the old trial trip, some fool comes in and interrupts you. What am I to do ?

LADY MAUD. Come and have a few holes of golf, and I'll rehearse you. (*Pulling* REGGIE *up.*)

REGGIE (*rising*). I'm awfully sorry, but I think I must stick about here for a bit. I have an appointment. At least I may have. But I'll take you for a run down the road in the car this afternoon. I have to return a spare rim.

LADY MAUD (*going* R. *and still holding* REGGIE's *hand*). Remember I'm confined to barracks. (*Turns.*) But who gave you a spare rim ?

REGGIE. An unknown sportsman who's staying at a cottage down there. I burst a tyre just outside his gate this morning, and he treated me like a prince. Sent his man out to fix the rim on, and gave me a cocktail under which I am still tingling.

LADY MAUD. Did he give Percy one ?

REGGIE. No; Percy was asleep in the back seat. I didn't show him. Kinder not, I thought.

LADY MAUD. And what was this Samaritan's name ?

REGGIE. He didn't tell me. He only took the cottage last night, he says. Down here for a quiet time.

(MISS FARADAY *appears, coming downstairs.*)

Oh—I say !

LADY MAUD. Is that your appointment ?

REGGIE (*gulping*). Yes.

LADY MAUD. I thought so. I'm off to the garden. (*Picking up her golf clubs—running out by window, laughing.*)

MISS FARADAY. Good morning, Mr. Reggie.

(REGGIE *develops elephantiasis at once—he rises awkwardly.*)

REGGIE. What-ho! Cheero. Hallo! H'm! (*Helplessly.*) What-ho!

MISS FARADAY. So you've got back from town ?

REGGIE (*gulping*). Yes.

MISS FARADAY. Did you bring Lord Totleigh back ?

REGGIE. Yes.

MISS FARADAY. Well, I must run and find Lord Marshmoreton. He wants me. (*Going towards the window.*)

REGGIE (*following her, with rigid limbs, getting in her way*). No he doesn't. He's taken a day off. Ha-hum! I say, come out into the garden and—and look at the crops. Wouldn't that be fun ?

MISS FARADAY. I don't think so.

REGGIE. Oh! (*Trying again.*) Do you go in for racing at all ?

MISS FARADAY. No.

REGGIE. Oh! Quite! You've never seen a Two-Thirty, I suppose ? I mean—it must be wonderful to win a packet—a baggage—a prize! Win a real prize. The absolute goods! *You* understand.

MISS FARADAY (*looking up at him*). Do I ?

(REGGIE *is evidently nerving himself for a final effort when enters* KEGGS *at door* L.)

REGGIE. Go away!

KEGGS. The tourists are waiting in the outer hall, Mr. Reggie. May I bring them in ?

(*Exit* MISS FARADAY *quietly* R. *upstairs.*)

REGGIE. No! Yes! I suppose so.

(*Exit* KEGGS *by door* L.)

Let's go into the garden, Miss Faraday. (*Turns.*) She's gone! (*Angrily.*) Another false start. As you were!

(*Exit by windows* C.)

(*Enter* KEGGS *by door* L. *He carries a long white wand.*)

KEGGS. Step this way, if you please, and kindly keep in line.

(*Enter* GOVERNESS *and two* CHILDREN, MAN *in black sombrero,* COCKNEY *and* WIFE, GEORGE BEVAN. KEGGS *stands at the door as they pass in, then closes it. The* MAN *in the sombrero goes straight to the fireplace, strikes a match on the mantelpiece, and tries to light a pipe.)*

No smoking, if you please; and kindly keep outside this rope. *(Edging the* MAN *away from the fireplace, and picking up the loose end of the rope, and hooking it to the wall.)*
MAN IN SOMBRERO. Snob !

(The COCKNEY *meanwhile has crossed* R. *to a figure in armour. This he raps with his stick, making a hollow sound.)*

COCKNEY *(to his wife).* 'Ere, Emma. 'E could do with a square meal.

(The CHILDREN *giggle.)*

KEGGS *(indignantly pointing to cardboard).* May I draw your attention to that notice ?
COCKNEY. Sorry, old sport !
KEGGS *(after glaring at them).* We are now in the Main Hall——
COCKNEY. Eh, what ?
KEGGS *(moving to* L.C.). We are now in the main 'all, and before going further I wish to point out to you the portrait by Sir Peter Lely of the Fifth Countess. Said to be in his best manner.
MAN IN SOMBRERO. Rotten.
GOVERNESS. In his best manner, Charlotte.
CHARLOTTE. I don't care—— *(In a sing-song voice.)*
KEGGS *(coming* C. *and pointing out to audience).* I should next like to draw your attention to this truly colossal group by an unknown artist, representing an assemblage of old English comedy types. Note the gargoyle-like effect of the faces in the foreground and the wide open mouths in the middle distance.
BILLIE *(entering from door* L.). Say, am I too late to connect with this rubbering outfit ?
KEGGS. I'm sorry, Madam ; this party is made up. I shall be taking a second party round in half an hour.
BILLIE *(appealingly).* Oh, let me in on this one. I've only got twenty minutes to spare.
KEGGS. You are not one of the charabanc party, Madam ?
BILLIE. No, I was just rolling by in a Royce.

(Sensation. All turn and look at BILLIE.)

MAN IN SOMBRERO. Pah !
BILLIE. It broke down on us outside your front gate, and my boy friend is underneath. He'll be through in less than half an hour. Can I stick around ? *(Very sweetly.)* Please, Lord Marshmoreton.
KEGGS *(trying hard not to show gratification).* Madam, you may remain.

BILLIE. Fine! I'll get in the bread line. (*Moving to* R. *and finding* GEORGE *at the tail of the line.*) Why, for goodness sake, George.

GEORGE (*rather furtively*). Hallo, Billie!

BILLIE. George, this is grand. But what are you doing here?

(KEGGS *is waiting, with a pained expression and bumping on the ground with wand.*)

Pardon me!

KEGGS. I should now like to call your attention to the piece of tapestry over the mantelpiece. It is Gobbling.

COCKNEY. Greedy! Greedy!

(KEGGS *glares at him and moves to* R.)

BILLIE. But, George, why are you hiding, anyway? Why did you walk out on us, and leave the show flat?

GEORGE. I'm staying here, at a little cottage down the road. I only took it last night.

BILLIE. But what's the idea? What made you choose this neck of the woods?

KEGGS (*taps brass stay with wand—coldly*). I am waiting, Madam.

(GEORGE *looks at stay closely.*)

BILLIE (*with a smile*). I'm sorry, officer. (*Holding up both her hands.*) Shoot when ready!

KEGGS. I will now call your attention to this large window with embattled terrace beyond—known in the family tradition as the scene of Lord Leonard's Leap. (*Standing on stool* R. *of window.*) In the year seventeen hundred and eighty-seven, a young Scottish nobleman, Lord Leonard Strathbungo, eldest son of His Grace the Duke of Gorbals——

BILLIE (*to* GEORGE). Ain't he cute?

KEGGS (*raising his voice*). Eldest son of His Grace the Duke of Gorbals, hurled himself out of this window to avoid compromising himself with the beautiful Countess of Marshmoreton—

(GOVERNESS *removes both* CHILDREN *towards* L. *with horrified expression*—CHILDREN *disappointed.*)

with whom he is related to have had a romance of a perfectly innercent character.

(*The* GOVERNESS *is reassured and they return to* C.)

I will now ask you to step out on to the terrace in order to observe the extent of the drop. Kindly keep in line.

(*All go out through the window except* GEORGE *and* BILLIE.)

BILLIE. But, George, you can't stay here. We want you at

the theatre. That Hot Potato number went blah the second night, and you've got to come back and fix it.

GEORGE. I've got other things to fix first. I must stay here, Billie.

BILLIE. Well, I can't altogether blame you. This is the life. Gee! Flowers and cows, and Leonard's Leaps, and everything.

(The Party begin to return.)

Oh, here's that spellbinder in the boiled shirt again. Let's beat it, George.

(They go out L.)

KEGGS. Kindly keep in line. *(Resuming.)* Having looked over the battlements, you will now be in a position to realize the hazardous nature of Lord Leonard's Leap.

COCKNEY. Did he break his neck, mister? *(Eagerly.)*

KEGGS. His lordship was fortunate enough to be caught in the branches of a cedar tree below, and thus escaped with a few 'armless contusions.

(Gratification all round, except from the MAN IN THE SOMBRERO.)

(Giving him a glance.) We will now proceed by way of the Amber Droring Room to the Long Gallery, once the scene of much mediaeval revelry, now occasionally used by the house party for amusing romps after dinner. Thereafter you will have the opportunity of inspecting certain of the bedrooms——

GOVERNESS *(rather horrified).* Bedrooms!

KEGGS. Under the personal ægis of Mrs. Popplewell, the housekeeper. Kindly keep in line.

(He goes upstairs, followed by the others. BILLIE and GEORGE re-enter L.)

BILLIE. Well, we side-stepped that. Now what?

GEORGE. I have a little private affair to attend to.

BILLIE. So you said. What's her name?

GEORGE *(rapturously).* Maud.

BILLIE. I never heard you speak a girl's name like that before, Georgie. Have you fallen at last?

GEORGE. Crashed!

BILLIE. You really love her?

GEORGE. I worship her.

BILLIE. Well, good luck, boy. *(Shaking his hand warmly.)* You deserve a good one. You're an ace, Georgie.

GEORGE. Thank you, Billie!

BILLIE. Does she live right here, in this ruin?

GEORGE *(looking through doors R., etc., for traces of LADY MAUD).* That's what I've come to find out.

(LORD MARSHMORETON *appears outside the window again, smoking, with more whale-oil, and gets busy at his tub of roses.*)

BILLIE. Well, don't let me detain you. Go right ahead with your treasure hunt. I'm just wild to get down into that garden and smell the roses. (*Turning and seeing* LORD MARSHMORETON'S *back view.*) Hello, there's a gardener. Do you think he'd show me around, for a dollar?

GEORGE. No harm in trying.

BILLIE (*going to window*). Hello, Dadda. How are the crops?

(LORD MARSHMORETON *turns and scowls at her, then seeing a charming girl, the frown clears away. He straightens himself, takes his pipe out of his mouth, and grins.*)

Don't stop smoking on my account. I like it. Well, what are you hunting with that soup-gun?

LORD MARSHMORETON. Thrips, Miss.

BILLIE. You have them in this old country, too, do you?

LORD MARSHMORETON. Yes, da—drat 'em, Miss!

BILLIE. That's too bad. Still, this certainly is the right sort of job that you are holding down here. If I was a man there's nothing I should like better than to work in a rose garden. Did you grow all those yourself?

LORD MARSHMORETON. Yes, Miss.

BILLIE (*looking over parapet*). And you sure have been a busy boy. All the fifty-seven varieties.

LORD MARSHMORETON. There are more than three thousand varieties.

BILLIE. Sure. I was only letting off one of our national cracks. You can't tell me anything about roses, Dadda. I'm the guy that invented them. Got any Ayrshires?

LORD MARSHMORETON. Ayrshires? You know about Ayrshires?

BILLIE. Sure I know.

LORD MARSHMORETON (*taking her arm*). Come with me. (*Leading her off.*)

BILLIE. Good-bye, Georgie. I got a Dadda at last!

(GEORGE *stands watching* LORD MARSHMORETON *and* BILLIE *as they pass out of sight.* ALBERTINA *appears furtively at the open door* L. *She enters mysteriously and stands gaping at him.* GEORGE *copies her.*)

GEORGE. Good morning!

ALBERTINA. Hush! Not so loud!

GEORGE (*taking* ALBERTINA *down stage, then in a whisper*). Sorry. Is somebody dead?

ALBERTINA (*whispering*). No, but I've guessed who you are.

c

GEORGE. Have you? Let me guess too. (*Shouting.*) *Who am I?*

ALBERTINA (*starting with fright*). You're Mr. X, and I'm your friend.

GEORGE (*backing away nervously*). I'm no such thing, and I don't think you're quite right in the head.

ALBERTINA. I've drawn you in a sweepstake.

GEORGE (*jumps*). *What?*

ALBERTINA. We've got one up about who Lady Maud's going to marry. If you marry her, I win.

GEORGE. Marry? Lady Maud? (*Dazed.*) But, my good girl, you don't even know my name.

ALBERTINA. It doesn't matter; you're The Field— (GEORGE *starts.*) Mr. X—and I'm going to help you.

GEORGE. Help me? You mean it? (*An idea begins to strike him.*)

ALBERTINA (*coming* L.). Of course I mean it. Do you think I'm going to let old Keggs win?

GEORGE. The boy orator?

ALBERTINA. He's my uncle, and he's drawn the favourite.

GEORGE. He would. But is Lady Maud here?

ALBERTINA. Yes, but they're keeping a close eye on her, because of you.

GEORGE. Because of me?

ALBERTINA. Yes. You needn't pretend with me, you know,—(*with a smile*)—I know why you're here.

GEORGE. Forgive my curiosity, but how do you know?

ALBERTINA. I couldn't help hearing what you said to that foreign young lady just now. I happened to be outside the door at the time.

GEORGE. I thought I heard something flapping. (*Indicating her ear.*) And you're really out to help me?

ALBERTINA. Of course. How am I going to put it across Uncle Albert if I don't?

GEORGE. Will you give Lady Maud a note for me?

ALBERTINA. Have you written it?

GEORGE. No.

ALBERTINA. Then do it now.

GEORGE. Right! (*He goes to the small table up* L. *and scribbles a note.*)

ALBERTINA (*crossing to* R.). One thing; we shall have to get you in here for the ball.

GEORGE (*still writing*). When is that?

ALBERTINA. On Toosday. Keggs thinks things will come to an 'ead that night. All the other runners will be here; and so must you be, or I'm sunk. We must manage it somehow. Have you got a dress suit?

GEORGE. No—not here.

ALBERTINA. A dickey, then ?

GEORGE. No.

ALBERTINA. Well, I might borrer one. Anyhow——

(*Voices are heard outside the window.*)

Crikey, I must 'op it. So long ; I mustn't be caught in 'ere with you. (*Running out L.*)

GEORGE. Here, wait a minute ! I've just finished the——

(*Enter* LORD MARSHMORETON *and* BILLIE, *chatting in most friendly fashion.* BILLIE *is carrying a large armful of roses.*)

BILLIE. 'Lo, Georgie. Look what Dadda has given me. And I'm going to have more ; he's got my address. Isn't he too lovely ? (*To* LORD MARSHMORETON.) You're sure you won't get fired for doing this ?

LORD MARSHMORETON. I'll risk it, Miss.

BILLIE. What sort of a hard-boiled egg is this old Earl of yours ?

LORD MARSHMORETON. Soft in spots, Miss.

BILLIE. Well, give him my love, and tell him you're a real gardener. Now I must beat it ; my boy friend under the car will be getting peevish. (*She slips a rose into the top of* LORD MARSH-MORETON'S *green apron.*) For you, Dadda.

LORD MARSHMORETON. Thank you, dear—Miss !

GEORGE. I'll come with you. I'm looking for some one. I wonder why she ran off like that.

BILLIE. Who—Maud ?

GEORGE. No, somebody else.

BILLIE (*moving to door L.*). Good-bye, Dadda. Keep right on after those thrips. (*Exit L.*)

(*Suddenly* GEORGE'S *eye falls on* LORD MARSHMORETON, *who is gazing after* BILLIE.)

GEORGE (R.C.). Look here, my man.

LORD MARSHMORETON (C., *turning*). Eh ?

GEORGE. You're still a young man, aren't you ? Still human.

LORD MARSHMORETON. I'm round about fifty, sir.

GEORGE. Nonsense ! You don't look a day over forty. The prime of life. I expect you know what it is to be in love, anyhow. And look at your figure—a mere boy.

LORD MARSHMORETON. Do I ?

GEORGE. Of course you do. In that case you can sympathize with me. Now,—(*handing him the note*)—see that Lady Maud gets this right away, there's a good chap. It's rather urgent.

(LORD MARSHMORETON *takes the note, slightly dazed.*)

And—er—(*handing him a pound note*)—thank you so much.

BILLIE (*calling from off* L.). Georgie!

GEORGE (*crossing to* L.). Coming! (*Turning back to* LORD MARSHMORETON.) I'll be back for an answer. Thank you so much.

LORD MARSHMORETON (*looking at the note and the pound, and then after* GEORGE). Well, I'm damned! (*Grinning and chuckling. Finally opening the note and reading it.*) Well, I *am* damned!

(*He is divided between wrath and amusement.*)

(*Enter* LADY CAROLINE *from the staircase* R.)

LADY CAROLINE. Have those tourists gone?

LORD MARSHMORETON. No; they're upstairs. Read that. (*Looking to* L. *after* GEORGE.)

LADY CAROLINE (*taking the note and reading it*). " If I can serve you in any way, let me know. I have taken Ivy Cottage, just down the road. I expect you can guess who I am." Whom is this addressed to? You?

LORD MARSHMORETON (*testily*). Don't be a fool, Caroline. To Maud.

LADY CAROLINE. And who wrote it?

LORD MARSHMORETON (*triumphantly*). The man from Switzerland. And he gave it to me. (*Chuckling again.*)

LADY CAROLINE. To you?

LORD MARSHMORETON. For Maud.

LADY CAROLINE. And he's here?

LORD MARSHMORETON. He was a minute ago. He's taking Miss—(*pausing—hesitating*)—Dore to her car.

LADY CAROLINE. Miss who?

LORD MARSHMORETON. She's one of the tourists. A nice, sensible girl. (*Forgetting all about* LADY MAUD.) Do you know, she actually told me something about hybrid perpetuals that I hadn't known before?

LADY CAROLINE. Harry, is this a moment to talk about hybrid perpetuals?

LORD MARSHMORETON. But I tell you she is the most sensible girl I ever——

LADY CAROLINE. Harry, your own daughter is in grave peril. Think! Think! At this moment she may be——

(*Enter* REGGIE *by window.*)

Reggie, my boy, thank Heaven you are here. The man from Switzerland is in this house, hunting for Maud. What are we to do? Think! Speak!

REGGIE (*after thinking*). What-ho!

LADY CAROLINE. But what steps are we to take?

REGGIE. Throw him out—what?

LADY CAROLINE. But where is he ? And where's Maud ?

REGGIE. She's playing golf, out there. But how did this fellow get in ?

LADY CAROLINE. With the tourists, I expect.

REGGIE. And now he's loose about the grounds somewhere—eh ?

LADY CAROLINE. Yes.

(*Enter* GEORGE L.)

LORD MARSHMORETON. No, damme ! Here he is again.

GEORGE (*looking round and smiling pleasantly*). Good morning ! I'm afraid I'm intruding on a family chat.

REGGIE. Ah, the spare rim. (*Recognizing him.*) Intruding ? Not on your life. Come in. (*Shaking* GEORGE *warmly by the hand.*) Jolly glad to see you. That cocktail hasn't worn off yet. What was it called ?

GEORGE. The Kicking Fish.

REGGIE. And what are you called ?

GEORGE. George Bevan.

LADY CAROLINE (*in an undertone to* LORD MARSHMORETON). His name's George Bevan.

GEORGE. Will you introduce me ?

REGGIE. Mum, this handsome stranger saved your baby boy's life not an hour ago. A spare rim and a Kicking Fish. (*To* GEORGE.) George, meet the baby's mother.

(GEORGE *bows*—LADY CAROLINE *glares at him.* GEORGE *turns, to find* LORD MARSHMORETON *at his elbow.*)

GEORGE (*under his breath*). Did you give it to her ?

LORD MARSHMORETON. No.

GEORGE. Why not ?

LORD MARSHMORETON (*shouting*). You infernal idiot, I'm her father.

GEORGE (*pulling the pound note out of* LORD MARSHMORETON'S *apron pocket*). Then give me back that Bradbury, Dadda.

LORD MARSHMORETON (*furiously*). T'chah ! (*Stamping up to window.*)

REGGIE (*roaring with laughter*). You—thought he was th-th-the gardener ?

GEORGE (*also roaring with laughter*). Ye-ye-yes !

REGGIE. Oh, my lord ! (*They both laugh together.*)

LADY CAROLINE. Silence, both of you !

REGGIE. But, Mum, this fellow's all right. He isn't the least like what we expected, is he ? He's short-haired ! He's clean ! He's human—almost ! I'm for him, and for Maud too ! Uncle Harry, why not let them marry each other ? He's potty about her, and she's crazy about him.

GEORGE. *What* did you say ?

REGGIE. Maud thinks your name is Lancelot and Galahad, Limited. Surely you know that. She must have told you herself.

LADY CAROLINE. It is only a foolish infatuation on her part.

LORD MARSHMORETON. She only thinks she's in love with you, damn it !

REGGIE. My dear old things, play the game ! (*To* GEORGE.) You should have heard her go off the deep end about you on the golf course just now. She said you were like the old fellow over there,—(*indicating knight in armour*)—pushing over the portcullis, and leaping this moat, and so forth, just to be able to hand her one glad look.

GEORGE. In that case, I'll come to the point at once. Lord Marshmoreton, I am very sorry I have made that rather natural mistake just now——

LORD MARSHMORETON (*sarcastically*). Don't mention it.

GEORGE. Right ! Then may I marry your daughter, please ?

LORD MARSHMORETON (*shouting*). No, you may not !

GEORGE. If not, why not ? Dadda, who gave you that rose ?

LORD MARSHMORETON (*going up stage*). Caroline, you say something. I think I'm going to burst.

LADY CAROLINE. The presumption of it ! Do you know that there were Marshmoretons in Totleigh before the Wars of the Roses ?

GEORGE. Do you know there were Bevans in Battersea before the Dog's Home ? Anyhow, Maud and I love each other, and we're willing to wait.

LADY CAROLINE (*to* GEORGE). Leave this house, please !

GEORGE. I'm going to. But I shall return, early and often. Good day, Lady Caroline. Good day, Lord Marshmoreton. So long, Reggie. (*Has moved up and is now at door* L.)

(PERCY *enters, on stairs.*)

(*Turning.*) My old friend Percy ! Did you get your hat back ? (*Moving back to* L.C.)

PERCY. Yes, I did ; and now you're going to pay for it. (*Crosses to* C.)

GEORGE. Oh ! How much ?

PERCY. About three months' hard, I hope.

GEORGE. For what, Percy ?

PERCY. Aggravated assault on me, and attempted abduction of my sister. How will you like that ?

(KEGGS *enters and is coming downstairs.*)

GEORGE. Three months ? And when is all this going to happen ?

PERCY. Now. I'm going to send for the police. (*Crossing* GEORGE *to the door* L.)

GEORGE. Oh ! Thanks for the warning, Percy. (*Crossing to* C.)

PERCY.   Keggs, guard those doors.   (*Indicating doors* R.)

KEGGS.   Very good, my lord.   (*Standing with his back to them and his arms extended.*)

(GEORGE *moves to* L.)

PERCY (*standing before door* L.).   And you shall pass through this door over my dead body, sir !

GEORGE.   Sorry I can't wait so long ; I must go some other way.

PERCY.   You try !

(FOOTMEN *appear* R. *and* L. *of the window.*)

Now, how are you going to get out ?

GEORGE.   By a way you would never have thought of, Percy. Maud would, though.

(*Enter* LADY MAUD, *by window, with golf clubs.*)

And here she is.   (*Moving to her.*)   Maud, my darling!   Never mind those things!   (*He takes the golf clubs from her and throws them on to* PERCY'S *toes.   Then he takes* LADY MAUD *in his arms.   She is too astonished to resist.*)   Au revoir, dear !   (*Before anyone can interfere he kisses* LADY MAUD.   *Then he turns and runs out by the window to the battlements.*)   Leonard's Leap !

(*He vaults over the battlements and disappears.*)

(LADY MAUD *gives a cry, and runs and leans over.*   PERCY *and the others follow.*)

(KEGGS *alone remains on duty before the door* R.   *Enter* L. ALBERTINA.   *She flaps her sweepstake ticket at him.*)

ALBERTINA.   Mr. X !   It's a walk over !

(*Running quickly off again.*)

CURTAIN.

ACT II

The SCENE *is the same as Act I, except that* PERCY'S *coming-of-age ball is now in progress. The rope, notices, etc., have disappeared. There is a table rigged up as a refreshment bar, and there are the usual ball decorations, banks of flowers, etc.*

GEORGE, *in footman's clothes, is at the table up* R.C., *with his back turned.*

(As the CURTAIN *rises, the guests are grouped* R., *half in and half out of the ball-room, facing towards* LORD MARSHMORETON, *who is standing on the settee* R.C. LADY CAROLINE, PERCY, REGGIE *and* LADY MAUD *are grouped round him. A clock up the stairs is striking twelve. All are listening. When the clock ceases—)*

LORD MARSHMORETON *(clearing his throat, and speaking without enthusiasm).* Well, everybody, you've all heard that clock strike twelve, and you all know what it means.

REGGIE *(solemnly).* It means it's to-morrow.

(Cries of " Sh ! ")

LORD MARSHMORETON *(after scowling at* REGGIE*).* It means that my son Percy is now twenty-one.

(Applause.)

I'm not going to make a speech about him, because I want you all to enjoy yourselves. So we'll just drink his health, and wish him long life—and happiness——

REGGIE. And a new hat !

(Cries of " Sh ! ")

LORD MARSHMORETON. —and as successful a future as his friends can reasonably expect of him. *(Lugubriously.)* Now then—hip hip——

ALL. Hooray ! Hooray !

*(*LORD MARSHMORETON *descends and goes* L.*)*

Hooray ! " He's a jolly good fellow " (8 *bars sung here*). Percy ! Dear old Percy ! etc. Speech !

*(*ALL *drink.* LADY MAUD *and* LADY CAROLINE *kiss* PERCY. *He*

40

goes down among the guests, shaking hands and being kissed.
Keggs *and* Albertina *collect empty glasses and take them up to
the table.* Reggie *hoists* Percy *on to the settee* R. *by stairs.*)

Reggie. Silence for the Vis—count !
Percy. Ladies and gentlemen——
Reggie. Bravo, bravo !
Percy (*giggles inanely*). I really don't know what to say at all.
Reggie. That's all right, old boy. I'll do all the talking.
(*Displacing* Percy *and standing on settee himself.*) My lords, ladies,
gentlemen——
All. Reggie ! Order ! Silence for Reggie !
Reggie. My lords, ladies and gentlemen——
Lord Marshmoreton. Shut up, Reggie.
Reggie. . . . and gentlemen—faithful old retainer—dear little
Albertina——

(Lady Caroline *puts her hand on his arm.*)

Percy is a stout fellow—(*laughter all round*)—might be a bit stouter,
but that will come in time.
Lady Caroline. Reggie, darling, do lower your voice.
Reggie. I can't, Mum ; I'm a tenor. To you here assembled,
old Perce is just another of those rollicking, loose-limbed, care-free
sprigs of our ancient—you-know-what-I-mean. But I tell you he
is something more. He is a public man—he is the man of the
moment. What has our Percy done within the last three days ?
What did he achieve only last Sunday ? He pushed Steve
Donoghue and Tallulah Bankhead—(*or other celebrities*)—right off
the front page of " The News of the World " and occupied it
himself ! Boys—girls—I give you Percy, the Prince of Policemen
Punchers ! (*Drinks.*)

(*Loud cheers and laughter. " He's a jolly good fellow " (8 bars
repeated), etc. Music strikes up in the ball-room and most of the
company troop off* R. Footman *closes the doors* R. Lord Marshmoreton, Lady Caroline, Lady Maud, Percy, Reggie, *the*
Dean of Dumbleton, *and his* Wife, *and* Lady Prudence
*remain. One or two couples go on to the terrace and look over the
battlements, etc.*)

(Keggs *goes out by door* L.)

(Albertina *joins* George, *who still keeps his back turned, and helps
him to polish glasses, etc.* Lord Marshmoreton *and* Lady
Maud, *arm in arm with* Percy, *go* L. *and talk.* Lady Prudence
and the Dean's Wife *go up to the table and drink hock-cup.* Lady
Caroline *goes down* R. *with the* Dean. Reggie *is looking anxiously
up the staircase, hoping to see* Miss Faraday. *His movements are
rather wooden.*)

Lady Caroline. Dean, will you speak to Reggie? The dear boy is evidently a little overstrung to-night?

Dean. So I was pained to observe.

Lady Caroline. I am sure that a word from you, as his god-father—you understand?

Dean (cooing). Surely, surely, dear Lady Caroline. (Going up a few stairs.) Reggie!

(Lady Caroline goes l. to the others.)

Reggie, dear boy. Just one moment, please.

Reggie. Yes, sir.

Dean. Don't you think you smoke too much?

Reggie. Smoke?

Dean. And drink as well?

Reggie. Quite as well, if not better. (They go upstairs together.)

Lord Marshmoreton. Can I go to bed now, Caroline?

Lady Caroline. Bed? Why?

Lord Marshmoreton. I'm tired. I've been away in London all day——

Lady Maud. And you were in London all yesterday, Daddy. What were you doing? Own up! You haven't been to London for months.

Lord Marshmoreton (uncomfortably—moving towards stairs). I was seeing about some roses. Good night!

Lady Caroline. You can't go to bed! We are going to have a real old-fashioned quadrille in a moment. You must lead off with the Dean's wife.

Lord Marshmoreton. Oh, my lord!

Lady Caroline. I shall take the Dean, and Percy Lady Prudence. That leaves Reggie for you, Maud dearest.

Lord Marshmoreton. Well, I'm damn well going to bed after that.

Lady Maud. You can if you like, Daddy, but I'm afraid you won't be very comfortable.

Lord Marshmoreton. What do you mean by that?

Lady Maud. You'll see when you get upstairs, darling.

Lord Marshmoreton. I warn you all, there are limits to human patience. (Moving up to table r.c.) Champagne!

(Albertina hands him a glass. Lady Prudence and the Dean's Wife come down l. and talk to Lady Maud and Lady Caroline. Meanwhile the Dean has been talking to Reggie. They now come downstairs.)

Dean. Then I have your promise, my dear godson? Cocoa hereafter!

Reggie. My dear bean—Dean! I'm so sorry. Cocoa it shall

be. But not until another dawn has broken. (*Solemnly.*) There's
a reason !

DEAN. A reason, dear boy ?

REGGIE. Yes. You remember in the War, if there was going
to be dirty work just before dawn, everybody was served out with
a double spot of rum ? Well, that's the reason. I can't tell you
more than that, except that I'm going to deliver a massed attack
this very a.m. to the success of which cocoa would be fatal.

(*The music strikes up off* R.)

Good night ! God bless ! (*Shaking him solemnly by the hand and
going upstairs again.*)

LADY CAROLINE. There's the quadrille music. All ready, everybody ? Harry !

(LORD MARSHMORETON *hastily finishes his glass, and offers his arm
and exits* R. *reluctantly with the* DEAN'S *wife.*)

Reggie !

(REGGIE, *much annoyed, turns and comes down.* LADY MAUD *takes
his arm, smiling. He immediately recovers his good temper. They
go out together.* PERCY *goes out with* LADY PRUDENCE, *a pretty
girl.* LADY CAROLINE *and the* DEAN *go out last. Other couples
appear from the terrace and from under the stairs and go out
after them.* FOOTMAN *closes the doors.* GEORGE *and* ALBERTINA
are left alone.)

(GEORGE *has his back still turned. He turns round. He is dressed
as a footman, and is disguised by a small moustache.*)

GEORGE. Is my moustache on straight, Albertina ?

ALBERTINA. No.

GEORGE. Then I'll take it off. (*Does so.*) Now, do you think
I came here to hand out hock-cup to half-wits *all* evening ? When
am I going to get a word with Lady Maud ?

ALBERTINA. She's been kept very busy. Remember all your
rivals is 'ere to-night. The entire field—and they've each got to
'ave a go.

(GEORGE *groans.*)

She's been took out on them battlements four times already to my
knowledge.

GEORGE. You gave her my note ?

ALBERTINA. Yes—when she was on 'er way to 'er bath before
dinner.

GEORGE. You swear it ?

ALBERTINA. Cut my throat if I tell a lie.

GEORGE. I certainly will.

(ALBERTINA *produces a crumpled sheet of paper.*)

Is that the answer ? Bless you, Albertina.

ALBERTINA. No, it's somethink I want to learn you—by 'eart.

GEORGE. What is it ?

ALBERTINA (*reading*). " 'Ints for the Young Lover." By Doctor Cupid.

GEORGE. *What ?*

ALBERTINA. I copied it from Aunt 'Ermiown's Page in " Weekly 'Eartease." I'll read it to you. (*Reading.*) " You cannot fail to succeed in your suet if you observe the following rules—triferling in themselves, but——"

GEORGE. What are the rules ?

ALBERTINA. " One. Seek her company on all occasions."

GEORGE. I'm doing that all right.

ALBERTINA. " Two. Be persistuent——"

GEORGE. Be what ?

ALBERTINA. Be—be—persy stewent. Faint 'eart——

GEORGE. I know that bit. Go on.

ALBERTINA. " Three. Ingratuate yourself with her relatives."

GEORGE. Thank you ; I've tried !

ALBERTINA. " Four. Play upon her natural affections. If she has a little brother, buy him sweetmeats and romp with him."

GEORGE. Percy ? I've tried romping with him already, but I'll buy him some jujubes to-morrow.

ALBERTINA. " Five——"

GEORGE. Is it all as helpful as this ?

ALBERTINA. Yes, nearly.

GEORGE. Then desist, Albertina ! My difficulty is not to find words, but to find the lady. Do you realize that the last time I saw her was in this room, last Thursday, just as I was preparing to jump out of that window ? What chance had I to say anything then ?

ALBERTINA. Still you found time to go a-kissing of her.

GEORGE (*thoughtfully*). Yes. That was just an impulse. I'm not quite sure that I was right to obey it. It didn't go with such a swing as I had hoped. I wasn't conscious of any come-back, so to speak.

ALBERTINA. There was a lot of people looking on. P'raps she was shy about kissing of you back.

GEORGE. Perhaps you're right. Anyhow, I don't leave this house till I see her.

(*Music stops. The doors* R. *open.*)

ALBERTINA. 'Ush ! They're coming back ! Put on your little moustache again. It's lying on top of the trifle.

(GEORGE *hastily resumes his moustache.*)

GEORGE. If you *can* catch Lady Maud alone, ask her if there's any answer to that note.

ALBERTINA. Righto!

(*Enter a couple.*)

MALE GUEST. But you can't get the real stuff here——

FEMALE GUEST. Oh yes, you can. That footman's a perfect lamb. He gave me a " gin and it " just now and had one himself. (*They go up to table, then out.*)

(*Enter* REGGIE *and* LADY MAUD.)

REGGIE (*who is not quite sober, but thinks that no one else knows ; solemnly*). Good old Lancers!

LADY MAUD. Reggie, dear, that was a quadrille.

REGGIE. Oh, was it ? I wondered, once or twice. Anyhow, it was one of those jolly things where you dance with somebody else's partner half the time.

LADY MAUD. More than that, in your case.

REGGIE. Well, you see, it was Alice! Dear little——! (*Begininng to stiffen and gape.*) Oh, my Lord, here she is.

(MISS FARADAY *comes out of the ball-room with* CAPTAIN PLUMMER. *She bows to him, and he goes out again.*)

LADY MAUD. What a lovely frock, Miss Faraday. Did you really make it yourself ?

MISS FARADAY. Yes.

REGGIE (*as solemn as ever*). Marvellous!

LADY MAUD. I wish I was as clever as you. Perhaps you're even clever enough to dance with Reggie. I'm not!

MISS FARADAY. Will you dance with me, Mr. Reggie ?

(REGGIE *makes an affectionate noise, crosses and gets into position.*)

LADY MAUD. Get me a glass of something first, Reggie dear. I'm dying of thirst.

(GEORGE, *who has been listening, eagerly hurries down with a glass of hock-cup.* LADY MAUD *takes glass without looking at him.* GEORGE *retires, furious.*)

(*Music strikes up again.*)

REGGIE (*to* MISS FARADAY). Now ?

MISS FARADAY. Yes. Aren't you dancing this, Lady Maud ?

LADY MAUD. No ; I'm going upstairs to hide.

MISS FARADAY. Hide ?

LADY MAUD. I don't think I can bear any more proposals to-night.

REGGIE. Does another impend ?

LADY MAUD. Yes. Captain Plummer. The worst yet. One of those strong silent proposers.

(REGGIE *makes a sympathetic noise.*)

MISS FARADAY (*to* REGGIE). Is that the man who shoots things ?

REGGIE. Yes. Whenever a girl turns him down, he goes to Central Africa and kills a hippopotamus.

LADY MAUD. Well, I'm going upstairs now—to save a hippo-potamus's life ! There can be very few of them left, poor things. Good-bye, Reggie ! Good luck ! (*Running upstairs.*)

REGGIE (*to* MISS FARADAY *with a great gulp*). Shall we ?

MISS FARADAY. Of course.

REGGIE (*ecstatically*). Ah !

(*They go out through the doors* R.)

GEORGE (*to* ALBERTINA *hurriedly*). Dash upstairs, and try to catch her now !

ALBERTINA. Righto, Mr. X. (*Running up the stairs and off.*)

(LORD MARSHMORETON *and* LADY CAROLINE *appear from the ball-room* R. *arguing—closing the doors* R.)

(*The Music stops.*)

LORD MARSHMORETON. Don't interrupt me, Caroline !

LADY CAROLINE. But, Harry——

LORD MARSHMORETON (*sitting down on the bottom step of the stairs*). You can Harry me till you're black in the face, but I'm going to have my say. Maud doesn't care a damn for Reggie and never will. There !

LADY CAROLINE (*sitting on a chair in front of staircase*). But she will learn, Harry ! Dear faithful Reggie will teach her. He's going to propose to her to-night.

LORD MARSHMORETON (*incredulously*). He said so ?

LADY CAROLINE. Well, he said it wouldn't be his fault if he wasn't engaged by two g.m. ! Dear, quaint boy.

LORD MARSHMORETON. I lay you a thousand to three Maud turns him down. She's in love with that young fellow George Bevan.

LADY CAROLINE. That creature ? We know nothing about him.

LORD MARSHMORETON. Don't we ?

LADY CAROLINE. What do you mean, Harry ?

LORD MARSHMORETON (*evasively*). Oh, nothing. But I know he's no fool. He's a good judge of men, for one thing. I found that out in my first talk with him. (*Giving a little gratified smile to himself.*) He's a stout fellow too ; he's got stuff in him. Look at the way he jumped out of that window the other day.

LADY CAROLINE. He ought to have broken his neck.

LORD MARSHMORETON. Yes, but he didn't. Just picked himself up, threw a kiss to Maud—or was it you?——

LADY CAROLINE. Really, Harry!

(GEORGE *laughs and exits through large window* o.)

LORD MARSHMORETON. —and strolled off as cool as be-damned. We shan't see him again, ·but I liked him. He's got nerve, that lad.

LADY CAROLINE (*acidly*). I'm not disputing that. To force one's way into a private house—into Totleigh Castle itself——

LORD MARSHMORETON (*rising*). My God, Caroline, you make me sick! You think the Marshmoretons are fenced off from the rest of the world by a sort of divinity. So does Percy. But Maud doesn't, bless her, and I wish her every kind of luck with her young man.

LADY CAROLINE. Harry, you've gone mad!

LORD MARSHMORETON. No, I've not. I'm just achieving sanity. I've lived in this atmosphere of snobbery and keep-off-the-grass-except-on-Thursdays until it has nearly choked me. (*Moving to* L.) I can't call my soul my own! The only two things I really care about are my daughter's happiness and growing roses. You're doing your best to mess up the one, and you won't even give me a chance to get on with the other. That infernal young woman—what's her name?—Faraday—she's a full-sized permanent blister in herself, and I'm through with her. She can take her accursed Family History and stuff it into the moat for all I care. I'm sick of this blue-blood business. I'm in prison here. For two pins I'd give the slip to the whole lot of you and go and live in London, in some little corner where no one would find me, and keep a flower-stall in Covent Garden Market, and mix with people who aren't stuck-up, mealy-mouthed snobs! There, I've said my say. Now I'm going to smoke a cigar outside, and then I'm going to bed. You can tell that prancing mob of spongers in there to go home—

[*Music (Fox Trot) starts again.*]

—if they've got any homes! And if they don't go soon, I'll come down with a syringe of whale oil and squirt it over the whole crawling crowd of them! Good night! (*Exit through window.*)

(LADY CAROLINE, *with a gesture of despair, goes out* R.)

(*Enter* GEORGE, *by window, looking after* LORD MARSHMORETON.)

GEORGE. That was a narrow one. Ooh! (*Helping himself to a drink.*)

(MISS FARADAY *and* REGGIE *enter from ball-room* R. GEORGE *hastily resumes his place.*)

Miss Faraday. But why do you want to stop dancing ? (*Closing the doors* R.)

(*Music stops.*)

Reggie. It's a rotten tune. (*Resolutely.*) Besides, zero hour is approaching.

Miss Faraday. What ?

Reggie (*weakening, suddenly*). Well, I mean—won't you come for a little walk and talk about the——?

Miss Faraday. Not the crops again—please, Mr. Reggie.

Reggie. Well then—spor—I mean—the two-thirt—— Anyhow, let us have a snifter before proceeding further. Cocoa to-morrow, but a man's drink to-day. What will you have ?

Miss Faraday (*rather meaningly*). Lemonade, please. (*Goes down to fireplace* L.)

Reggie (*to* George). Waiter, will you give me a lemonade for a lady, like a good chap.

George. Yes, sir. (*Beginning to pour lemonade into a glass.*) I'm sorry you didn't like that fox-trot.

Reggie. Why ?

George. I wrote it.

Reggie. That's damn good, old man ! You wrote it !

George. Say when !

Reggie (*laughing heartily*). When ! (*Taking the glass to* Miss Faraday, *then returning to* George *and after staring rather owlishly at him.*) I say, old man ?

George. Sir ? (*Pause.*)

Reggie. I haven't ever seen you before by any chance, if you know what you mean, have you ?

George (*solemnly*). No, sir.

Reggie. You haven't got a brother or anything in that shape or form, have you ?

George. No, sir. I often wish I had. I ought to have spoken to father about it. Father could never deny me anything.

Reggie. *What's that ?*

George. Sir ?

Reggie. What did you say ?

George. I said, " Yes, sir, I have no—brother."

Reggie. Didn't you say anything else ?

George. No, sir.

Reggie (*to himself*). Good lord ! Then that old gentleman was right. Cocoa hereafter. (*Going slowly towards* Miss Faraday.)

Miss Faraday. What were you talking to that man about, Mr. Reggie ?

Reggie. I asked him if he had a brother.

Miss Faraday (*rising*). A brother ? What made you ask him that ?

REGGIE. He—I mean to say—he looks like the sort of feller that might have a brother. Lots of these chaps have.

MISS FARADAY (*handing him the lemonade*). Mr. Reggie, I think perhaps you had better drink this.

REGGIE (*taking the glass*). I think perhaps you're right.

MISS FARADAY. Shall we go out on to the battlements? There's a nice breeze getting up.

REGGIE. Yes; I can feel it! (*Following her out by the window C.*)

GEORGE (*looking after him*). That ought to keep you out of the way for half an hour, old man.

(ALBERTINA *appears, running downstairs.*)

ALBERTINA. Sir, sir, she's a-coming! (*Coming down and crossing to L.*)

GEORGE (*flustered*). Is she? Oh lord! Very well! Get out of here like a good girl.

ALBERTINA. All right, sir. Take off that moustache, and be yourself; and remember, sir, be persistuent! (*Runs out by the door L.*)

(LADY MAUD *appears coming downstairs.* GEORGE, *having made himself look as presentable as possible, waits for her C. They stand face to face.*)

GEORGE (*almost reverently*). At last! Maud! (*Advancing a step.*)

(*She makes no movement. He pauses.*)

LADY MAUD. Mr. George Bevan, I want to speak to you. You are George Bevan, aren't you? Why have you dressed up like that?

GEORGE. To get in here. It was the only way I could see you.

LADY MAUD. But why do you want to see me? You don't even know me.

GEORGE. I may not know you, but I love you.

(*Music starts. Waltz here.*)

LADY MAUD (*taken aback, but recovering herself*). Then why did you jump out of that window? Were you frightened of Percy?

GEORGE (*imitating* PERCY's *voice*). No, I was not! (*Quietly.*) Shall I tell you the real reason? I had just kissed you, and I felt as if I could jump over the moon; but the moon didn't happen to be out at the moment, so I jumped over the battlements.

LADY MAUD. Oh! Did you hurt yourself?

GEORGE. I escaped with a few "'armless contusions."

LADY MAUD (*with a laugh*). I am glad and I am flattered.

GEORGE. Flattered?

D

LADY MAUD. Yes, it was rather a splendid compliment, you know. A girl appreciates that.

GEORGE. Maud——

(*Enter* CAPTAIN PLUMMER *from doors* R. *He is a large slow-moving man, with a solemn stare. Closing the doors* R.)

PLUMMER (*loudly*). My dance, Lady Maud, I think.

LADY MAUD. I am so sorry, Captain Plummer. Shall we go into the ball-room ?

PLUMMER. *No,* if you pleease ; up here !

(*They go upstairs together.* LADY MAUD *looks back.* GEORGE *makes a furious noise to himself.*)

(*Enter* ALBERTINA *furtively from* L.)

(*Music stops.*)

ALBERTINA. Well, sir, have you seen her yet ?

GEORGE (*going to her, whispering*). Yes, for about one minute.

ALBERTINA. Well,—(*whispering back*)—'oo is she with now ?

GEORGE. Captain Plummer.

ALBERTINA. Ah ! One of the laundry maids drew 'im. He won't finish in the first six !

(*The door opens* R., *and* PERCY *enters and closes doors.*)

GEORGE. Get out !

ALBERTINA (*smiling*). I'll come back !

(*Exit by door* L.)

PERCY. You—waiter !

(GEORGE *hastily turns away and puts on his moustache.*)

GEORGE (*turning to* PERCY). Yes, sir ?

PERCY. Sir !

GEORGE. My Lord ! Sorry !

PERCY (*after staring at* GEORGE *in a puzzled way*). Got any champagne ?

GEORGE. I'll see, my lord. (*Finding some.*) Yes, here we are, m'lord.

PERCY. Take a pint bottle up to my room—and one glass.

GEORGE. Yes, my lord. (*Taking up bottle and glass on small salver and moving to stairs.*)

PERCY. Stop !

GEORGE (*turning*). My lord ?

PERCY. I haven't seen you before, have I ?

GEORGE. No, my lord. I am only temporarily attached to the Castle staff.

PERCY. Where do you come from ? Where do you live ?

GEORGE. Devonshire Hou—Devonshire.

PERCY. Who engaged you ? Keggs ?

GEORGE (*chattily ; feeling he cannot be serious over* PERCY). Indirectly, my lord. My little step-niece, Albertina, the between-maid, introduced me to the housekeeper, Mrs. Popplewell, and Mrs. Popplewell recommended me to Mr. Keggs. I had not the pleasure of an actual interview with Mr.——

PERCY. Damn it all, do you think I want to hear the story of your life ?

GEORGE. Yes—no, my lord !

PERCY. Well, take that bottle upstairs !

GEORGE. Yes, my lord.

PERCY. And tell some one to find Keggs for me.

GEORGE. Yes, my lord.

(*Moving upstairs.* LADY MAUD *enters downstairs directly afterwards.*)

LADY MAUD. Well, Percy, darling, enjoying your party ?

PERCY. No. Why should I ?

(*Enter* CAPTAIN PLUMMER *downstairs, gloomily.*)

LADY MAUD. Poor Percy ! Prison life breaks the spirit. Never mind, supper will be ready in about ten minutes. I'm going to see about it now. You know Captain Plummer, don't you ? I must run. Au revoir, Captain Plummer !

(*Running off by doors* R., *which she closes after her.*)

PERCY. Hallo, Plummer.

PLUMMER. Hallo !

PERCY. Jolly good of you to come to this devastating party. Why did you ?

PLUMMER (*looking after* LADY MAUD). I don't know.

PERCY. I see. (*Moving towards* PLUMMER.) Not enjoying yourself by any chance, are you ?

PLUMMER. No.

PERCY. No. Have a drink ?

PLUMMER. Yes.

(PLUMMER *goes to table.*)

(*Enter* KEGGS *from* L.)

KEGGS. You sent for me, my lord ?

PERCY. Yes. But give Captain Plummer a drink first.

KEGGS. Yes, my lord. (*To* PLUMMER.) What can I give you, sir ?

PLUMMER. A baby soda.

KEGGS. Certainly, sir.

PLUMMER. And you can put two large brandies in it.

KEGGS. Yes, sir.

(GEORGE *appears coming downstairs.* KEGGS *turns to . him.*)

You—attend to this gentleman ! (*Going to* PERCY, *down* L.) I am
entirely at your disposal now, my lord.

PERCY. You've got a lot of extra waiters here to-night, haven't
you ?

KEGGS. Yes, my lord. The unprecedented scale of the enter-
tainment made temporary help imperative.

PERCY. Did you book them all yourself ?

KEGGS. Practically, my lord. I hope none of them has been——

PERCY (*pointing to* GEORGE, *who is pressing light refreshments upon*
PLUMMER). Do you know anything about that fellow ?

KEGGS. I don't seem to recognize him, my lord.

PERCY. He's the between-maid's grandfather, or something.

KEGGS (*smiling indulgently*). Hardly that, my lord, but I recol-
lect now.

(GEORGE *places a cigar in* PLUMMER'S *mouth and lights it for him.*)

The housekeeper asked my permission——

PERCY (*indignantly*). I say, look at that !

(GEORGE *has just handed* PLUMMER *another large drink and with his
hand on his shoulder now steers him out through the window.*)

GEORGE (*cheerily*). You go and sit on one of those deep chairs
along there, sir, and finish that, and in half an hour you'll be quite
looking forward to shooting rhinoceroses.

PLUMMER. Hippopotamuses, you fool !

GEORGE. To be sure, sir. You hit 'em both in the same place.
(*Following* PLUMMER *off* R.)

(PERCY *and* KEGGS *steal to the window and look after* GEORGE. *Then
they turn to one another.*)

KEGGS (*coming down again*). I have a feeling, my lord, that I
have encountered that person before.

PERCY. Feeling ? I'm certain ! It's that damn fellow who
jumped over the battlements last Thursday.

KEGGS. You mean—her young ladyship's unfortunate entangle-
ment, by lord ?

PERCY. Of course ! He's a poet from Switzerland.

KEGGS. Then hadn't we better take immediate steps, my lord ?

PERCY. Wait a minute ! We want to be sure. If it's the wrong
man, that'll make me look a fool twice in one week.

KEGGS. May I suggest an alternative plan, sir ? If he says
he's related to the between-maid, she must be cognizant of this.
I'll twist her ta—I will interrogate the young person, my lord.

PERCY. Right. (*Going up to top of stairs.*) I'm going up to
my room. Let me know as soon as you're certain, and I'll telephone
for a policeman. This time we've got the blighter. I hope they
bath *him* twice at Marlborough Street !

(*Exit from top of stairs.*)

(*Left alone,* KEGGS *moves up to the table and mixes himself a small
drink. While he is swallowing this, with his back turned and head
well back, the door* L. *opens and* ALBERTINA *appears.*)

ALBERTINA. Have you seen her yet, sir ? (*Recognizes* KEGGS,
and gives a yelp.)

KEGGS (*coming down and taking her by the shoulder*). A-a-ah !
(*Bringing her down* L.C.) Now, young blighted Albertina, I've got
you where I want you—at last ! (*Taking her by the shoulder, leading
her across and sits her on the arm of the chair at foot of stairs, and
standing over her.*) Now—(*with a fair imitation of* LORD MARSH-
MORETON'S *voice*)—what about all these new relations you've been
inventing—hey ?

(ALBERTINA *promptly falls backwards into the arm-chair, then sits up
slowly.*)

ALBERTINA. What about that ?

KEGGS. Who is he ? This grandfather or whatever you call
him ? That's what me and his young lordship have just been
asking ourselves. Who is he, really ? Come on !

ALBERTINA (*doggedly*). I don't know who you're talking about ?

KEGGS. Oh, don't you ? I'm talking about that common person
who's been hanging round Lady Maud for the last week. Have
you introduced him into these premises to-night, or have you not—
hey ?

ALBERTINA. I never !

KEGGS. Own up !

ALBERTINA. Well,—(*defiantly standing up*)—I'd a perfect right
to do what I could for my client.

KEGGS. What do you mean—client ?

ALBERTINA. You silly old fool, he's Mr. X ! Have you forgotten
that ? He's the runner I drew in the sweepstake. Him and Lady
Maud have been trying to get together all evening, and I've been
trying to help them. And who has a better right ? (*She is standing
up now, squarely facing* KEGGS.)

KEGGS. Lady Maud *wants* to see him ?

ALBERTINA. Why, she's 'alf out of 'er mind with love for 'im.
That's why I done what I done.

(KEGGS *is struck by an idea.*)

KEGGS. What's his name ?

ALBERTINA. I don't know.

KEGGS. Never mind; I'll find out. (*Thoughtfully.*) You say
Maud's made up her mind to marry this outsider?

ALBERTINA. Sure as death!

KEGGS (*promptly*). Then give me the Field—your Mr. X ticket
—and we'll call things square.

(ALBERTINA *gazes at him in speechless indignation.*)

Come on! Ticket or sack—whichever you prefer.

ALBERTINA. You pop-eyed old sharper!

KEGGS (*going towards the door* L.). We'll go into the matter
properly when I bring you up on the carpet before her ladyship
to-morrow.

ALBERTINA. You wouldn't go and do that, Uncle Albert?

KEGGS. Wouldn't I? Come on; hand over!

(ALBERTINA, *whimpering, pulls the ticket out of her dress, and gives
it to him.*)

Thank you.

ALBERTINA. Pincher!

KEGGS. Pincher, am I? Then I'll tell you what I'll do. I'll
give you back Reggie's ticket. There it is.

ALBERTINA. Thank you for nothing.

KEGGS. And I'll do more than that. I'll give you back the
Field as well.

ALBERTINA. You will?

KEGGS. I will. Bar one, of course. You'll admit the Field
belongs to me, by fair exchange? Very well. I'm going to make
one little selection out of that Field—just one—the Poet from
Switzerland! All the rest belong to you. (*Writing on his ticket.*)
Poet from Switzerland. I'll fill in his name when I get it. There!
I've scratched out the Field; now give me back that ticket of
yours for a minute. (*Taking it and writing on it.*) And Field.
(*Giving it back.*) No—don't thank me. All I want is the pleasure
of pouring coals of fire on your silly fat little 'ead.

(ALBERTINA *begins to go upstairs.*)

What are you going up them front stairs for?

ALBERTINA (*with dignity*). I am going up to the smoking-room
to see if I can find my new client.

KEGGS. Reggie?

ALBERTINA. Yes. If your measly poet jumps out of that window again, and breaks his neck—that's where I bring Reggie in,
to beat you on the post and rob you of your pound of flesh. So
long—Skylark! (*Exit haughtily from top of stairs.*)

(LORD MARSHMORETON *appears at the window* C., *looking off, as if
scrutinizing somebody. As he enters, he chuckles. He goes to the
foot of the stairs, where he encounters* KEGGS. *He starts slightly.*)

LORD MARSHMORETON. Good night, Keggs. I'm going to bed.
(*Goes up stairs.*)
KEGGS (*bowing*). Good night, my lord.

(LORD MARSHMORETON *has another look, through the window* R., *from over the banister, then goes upstairs with another chuckle.*)

(GEORGE *appears cautiously at window* C., *and enters. He finds himself face to face with* KEGGS.)

KEGGS. Might I have a word with you, sir ?
GEORGE. Me ?
KEGGS. Yes, sir. I penetrated your little disguise from the start, sir.
GEORGE (*annoyed*). Oh, did you ?
KEGGS. Yes, sir ; and may I take this opportunity of saying how warmly I sympathize with you in your romantic ambition.
GEORGE. But I thought you drew Reggie.
KEGGS (*starting slightly*). You were misinformed, sir.
GEORGE. Then you really think I'm the man for Lady Maud, Keggs ?
KEGGS. I know it, sir. And she knows it.
GEORGE. Have a drink ? (*Offering a bottle of champagne.*)
KEGGS. Righto ! (*Correcting himself, with a little cough.*) 1 thank you, sir. (*He pours out two glasses.*) Now, sir, I want to help you. Naturally, you would like an interview with Lady Maud.
GEORGE. The question is, would Lady Maud like to have an interview with me ?
KEGGS. Make no mistake about that, sir, her young ladyship's 'alf out of her mind with love for you.
GEORGE. You believe that too ?
KEGGS. I've known her from a little girl, sir. I can read her very thoughts.
GEORGE. Keggs, you give me fresh hope. But I can't get near her. She's entirely surrounded by Plummers.
KEGGS. Plumbers, sir ?
GEORGE. People proposing. Can't you insulate her for a few minutes ?
KEGGS. Certainly, sir. Listen. Supper will be announced directly. I'll get 'em all safely boxed in the dining-room, and then I'll bring Lady Maud in here for you.
GEORGE. You will ?
KEGGS. I will, sir.
GEORGE (*taking glass*). Keggs, your very good health !
KEGGS (*on his* L., *taking glass*). The same to you, sir, and success with her ladyship.
GEORGE. Thanks. God bless ! (*Drinking.*)
KEGGS. Skin off your nose, sir ! (*Drinking.*)

(ALBERTINA *appears from the stairs, watching them.* KEGGS *catches sight of her over the rim of his glass. They exchange glares.*)

Now, sir, you'd better come with me and straighten yourself up for the interview. I can get you a better coat than that—one of Reggie's. You must look your best.

(*They move over to the door* L.)

GEORGE. Keggs, you think of everything.

KEGGS (*reverently*). Particularly her young ladyship's happiness, sir.

(GEORGE *goes out by the door* L. KEGGS *glances up triumphantly at* ALBERTINA, *and goes out after* GEORGE.)

(ALBERTINA *scuttles downstairs and lands with a jump.*)

ALBERTINA (*crossing to* L.C., *looking after* KEGGS). You perishing old bodysnatcher! Oh, where's that Reggie?

(*Enter* REGGIE, *disconsolately, by window. She runs to him.*)

Ah, there you are, sir. There's no time to be lost.

REGGIE. Go away, and let me die quietly!

ALBERTINA. Die? You ain't going to die.

REGGIE (*angrily*). Yes, I am! There's nothing else to do.

ALBERTINA. Listen to me, sir! Do you want to marry the girl or don't you?

REGGIE. Of course I do! Don't be silly. But it's hopeless.

ALBERTINA. How do you know?

REGGIE. Because I can't ask her. I've just been trying for three-quarters of an hour, and it's no good.

ALBERTINA. You mean, you don't know how to set about her?

REGGIE. You've hit it.

ALBERTINA (*triumphantly producing* "Weekly Heartsease"). Then read this.

REGGIE. What is it?

ALBERTINA. "'Ints for the Young Lover, by Doctor Cupid." Aunt 'Ermiown! (*Pointing.*) Look! There! "Be persistuent! Faint 'eart, etcetera. Do not be tongue-tied. Carry her by a— (*turning over page*)—salt!"

REGGIE (*suddenly cheering up*). But, Albertina, this is marvellous! I've been looking for something like this for months. Give me half an hour to mug it up, and I'll have another dash! (*Taking the paper and going up.*)

ALBERTINA. You can't 'ave more than five minutes; it's urgent, I tell you.

REGGIE. What do you mean?

ALBERTINA. Never you mind! But you've got to do it now,

or lose her ! Run your eye over that once, and get down to it.
You'll find her in the ball-room.

REGGIE. No ; she's out on the terrace.

ALBERTINA (*pointing*). I tell you, she's there !

REGGIE. Out there !

(*The door* L. *is thrown open by a* FOOTMAN, *who crosses to* R. *and
opens the doors there. The* FOOTMAN *goes out* R.)

(*Music is heard. " The Roast Beef of Old England."*)

ALBERTINA. There's supper ; I must 'op it. But find 'er anyway. And carry 'er by a salt !

(*She scuttles upstairs again and* REGGIE *goes out on to the terrace* C.)

(*As the doors are closed the music stops ; there is a babble of voices
off* R. KEGGS *appears* L. *He turns to the outer hall behind him.*)

KEGGS. Supper is served ! (*Then goes to window.*) Supper is
served !

(*Music off. " Roast Beef of Old England," etc. A couple enter by
window and exit* R.)

KEGGS (*standing at the doors* R.). Supper is served ! (*Going up
to window.*)

(PLUMMER *and* MRS. MOSSOP *enter from window and go out* R. *Then
the* DEAN, *with* LADY PRUDENCE *and another girl, from* L. *They
go out* R., *talking.*)

(PERCY *appears on stairs.*)

PERCY. Here, Keggs.

(KEGGS *resolutely keeps his back turned, and stays outside the window.*)

(*Enter* LADY CAROLINE R.)

LADY CAROLINE. Percy dear, I want you to take Lady Prudence
in to supper.

PERCY. I can't. (*Coming down to* R.C.) I want to speak to
Keggs.

(*Enter* LADY PRUDENCE R.)

LADY CAROLINE. Here's Percy, Prudence, looking for you
everywhere.

LADY PRUDENCE. Percy dear, don't you want to take me in to
supper ?

PERCY. Oh, I'd love to.

LADY PRUDENCE. Then don't look so beastly pleased about it.

(PERCY, *much annoyed, goes out with* LADY PRUDENCE *by the doors* R.)

(KEGGS *appears from terrace.*)

LADY CAROLINE. Keggs, tell Mr. Reggie to find Lady Maud and take her in to supper.

(Exit by doors R., a FOOTMAN closing the doors.)

KEGGS. Yes, my lady. Tell Mr. Reggie to take Lady Maud in to supper ? I don't think ! *(Calling to REGGIE.)* Do you object if I close these windows for the present, Mr. Reggie ?

REGGIE *(off L.).* Go away !

KEGGS. Very good, sir. *(He comes in, closing the windows, then closing the door L.)*

*(*KEGGS *now crosses stealthily to the doors R., and opens one. LADY MAUD enters. They are now alone together.)*

LADY MAUD *(moving to C.).* Now, Keggs, what is all this mystery ?

KEGGS *(on her R.).* I hope your ladyship will forgive an old family servant for the liberty he has presumed to take.

LADY MAUD. Tell me what it is, and I'll see.

KEGGS. Your ladyship, I am not unaware that you have contracted an affection for a certain party—a poetical party——

LADY MAUD *(despairingly).* Is there anybody in this house who doesn't know my affairs ?

KEGGS. —which is more than reciprocated.

LADY MAUD. I am going to supper. *(Moving in front of KEGGS to R.)*

KEGGS. The party in question, my lady, has at last surmounted all obstacles—leaped all barriers——

LADY MAUD *(turning sharply).* He's here ? Mr. Austen Gray ? In this house ?

KEGGS. That very gentleman, my lady—Mr. Austen Gray. Love laughs at——

LADY MAUD. Never mind all that. Where is he ?

KEGGS *(pointing to door L.).* On the other side of that door, my lady, waiting. If you will give yourself the trouble of rapping on the panel, you'll get a delightful surprise. 'Ave I your permission to withdraw, my lady ?

LADY MAUD. Good gracious, yes ! *(Crossing to L.)*

KEGGS. I thank your ladyship.

(Bowing solemnly, and, as he goes out, he brings out his ticket and hurriedly writes on it.)

Mr. Austen Gray !

(Exit doors R., which he shuts.)

*(*LADY MAUD, *after a moment's hesitation, taps on the door L., then stands back and waits. Enter* GEORGE ; *he is wearing proper evening dress.)*

(Music off—" Blue Danube.")

LADY MAUD (*surprised and angry*). Mr. Bevan !
GEORGE (*a little taken aback*). Weren't you expecting me ?
LADY MAUD. No, I was not !
GEORGE. But Keggs——
LADY MAUD. Did you bribe Keggs to do this ?
GEORGE. With my hand on my heart, no ! Keggs did it off his own bat.
LADY MAUD. Why ?
GEORGE. He drew—— No, he didn't ! He swopp—I mean—he said your happiness was his only thought.
LADY MAUD. And Keggs thinks that you are my happiness ?
GEORGE. Yes, and Keggs isn't the only one.
LADY MAUD. Have other people been telling you that I—I—reciprocate ?
GEORGE. I should think they have !
LADY MAUD. Who ?
GEORGE. Your cousin Reggie, your father, your Aunt Caroline, and Albertina. Now Keggs. Fifty million people can't be wrong.
LADY MAUD. They can, if they've all made the same error. (*Crossing to* R.)
GEORGE. What error ?
LADY MAUD. They're mistaking you for some one else.
GEORGE. What ?

(LADY MAUD *moves to* R. *and sits on the stairs.—Pause.*)

LADY MAUD. Mr. Bevan, I'm going to pay you the rarest compliment a woman can pay a man. I'm going to tell you the truth. Will you sit down ?
GEORGE. I think perhaps I'd better. (*Sitting on settee.*)

(LADY MAUD *rises and stands* L. *of him.*)

LADY MAUD. You did me a very good turn the other day, and I owe you something for that. Besides, you really do seem to—to——
GEORGE. To be in earnest ?
LADY MAUD. Yes. I suppose that is why you have done all these rather—rather——
GEORGE. Ridiculous ?
LADY MAUD. Yes—ridiculous things.
GEORGE. Leonard's Leap—and that comic livery—and so forth ?
LADY MAUD. Anyhow, I think you're entitled to an explanation. When I took refuge with you the other day from Percy, I had come to town to keep an appointment—to see—(*very deliberately*)—the man I am engaged to. (*A pause.*)
GEORGE. Engaged ? (*Looking her full in the face.*)
LADY MAUD. Yes.

GEORGE. I see. (*Turning his head away to* R.) Go on, please.

LADY MAUD. His name is Austen Gray. I suppose you have heard of him ? (*Proudly.*) He's the poet.

GEORGE. Oh !

LADY MAUD. He's rather wonderful. He's very simple and idealistic, and dreamy—and rather tall and emaciated.

GEORGE (*gravely*). Oh ! You like them tall and emaciated ?

LADY MAUD. Not too emaciated. But not too chubby, either. I can't bear chubby men. I used to beg Austen to eat more. But he wouldn't. He said all food was gross and earthly; it killed inspiration. He said I was all the food he wanted. I suppose you think that silly and sentimental ?

GEORGE. I wish I'd thought of it.

LADY MAUD. Anyhow, that is what he was like, a year ago, and I haven't seen him since.

GEORGE. A year ago ? I suppose there's no chance of his having faded away altogether ?

LADY MAUD (*impatiently*). No, I have just told you—I had an appointment with him last Thursday.

GEORGE. Of course. Stupid !

LADY MAUD. He has been abroad for more than six months; he came back last week. That was why I went up to town to meet him.

GEORGE. But you didn't meet him.

LADY MAUD. No. Percy saw me; and if it hadn't been for you there'd have been a terrible scene.

GEORGE (*simply*). I'm proud that I was able to be of the smallest service.

LADY MAUD. You mean that ?

GEORGE (*looking at her steadily*). Absolutely.

LADY MAUD (*smiling*). I think you are rather a chivalrous person.

GEORGE. Not really chivalrous. I love you, that's all.

LADY MAUD (*moving slightly to* L.). But you mustn't go on saying that now.

GEORGE. All right. (*Rising and coming to her.*) I'll keep it to myself, but if there's anything I can do for you, at any time, that your poet can't do, let me know. Anything—at any time. I promise.

(GEORGE *and* LADY MAUD *stand gazing straight into one another's eyes.* LADY CAROLINE's *voice is heard outside.*)

LADY CAROLINE. I'm just coming. I must find Maud and Reggie for supper. They're hiding together somewhere, the naughty children.

(LADY MAUD *starts up and signs to* GEORGE *to go.*)

(GEORGE *goes up to windows* C. *and lets himself out.*)

(*As the windows close, the doors* R. *open and* LADY CAROLINE *enters.*)

Aren't you coming to supper, Maud ?
LADY MAUD. In half a minute, Auntie.
LADY CAROLINE. All alone, darling ?
LADY MAUD. I am at the moment.
LADY CAROLINE (*archly*). But you haven't been ?
LADY MAUD. No.
LADY CAROLINE. Could I guess who it was ?
LADY MAUD. Perhaps.
LADY CAROLINE. Have you any news for me, dear ?
LADY MAUD (*desperately*). I may have shortly, Auntie. In a day or two, perhaps.
LADY CAROLINE. Darling ! (*Kissing her.*) I must tell your father ! (*Going out doors* R. *with a parting smile.*) Oh, you naughty girl ! (*Shutting the doors after her.*)

(*Music stops.*)

(LADY MAUD *goes up to the windows and opens them, then comes down and waits.* GEORGE *re-enters.*)

GEORGE. Who was that ?
LADY MAUD. Aunt Caroline. She thought you were Reggie— and I let her ! In about five minutes she'll be announcing my engagement to him. That finishes everything. Oh, how I wish I had a brother like you instead of Percy ! Then he would help me. (*Crossing slowly down to fireplace.*)
GEORGE. Why shouldn't I help ?
LADY MAUD. You will ?
GEORGE. Of course. I promised.
LADY MAUD. Then tell me what to do.

(GEORGE *goes up to window, thinks, and comes down, his mind made up.*)

GEORGE. Have you courage ?
LADY MAUD. To do what ?
GEORGE. To burn your boats. To go to Austen Gray—now !
LADY MAUD. Now ?
GEORGE. Yes. Look—it's almost daylight. We'll take Reggie's car, and I'll run you straight up to town. Then you can talk matters over with the man you love. It's for him to advise you, not me. Can you get into touch with him anywhere ?
LADY MAUD. Yes. There's a teashop in Hanover Square where I can meet him any time. But you promise faithfully to stand by me—until——
GEORGE. Until everything is settled ? You bet I will !

LADY MAUD. Thank you—brother.

GEORGE. That's all right—sister !

*(They smile at one another with real friendship. There is a babble
of voices outside the doors R.)*

LADY MAUD. They're coming back ! Run and get a hat and
coat, and meet me out there. *(Indicating windows* C.*)* I shan't
be a moment. *(She runs to the foot of the staircase, but the door* R.
is opening. She runs back to him.)

GEORGE. You can't get upstairs now. Come with me ; I'll
find a wrap for you. *(Taking her hand ; they run out by the windows
and disappear.)*

(Enter LADY CAROLINE *with the* DEAN, PERCY *follows with* LADY
PRUDENCE, *then* MRS. MOSSOP *with* CAPTAIN PLUMMER, *who is
wrapped in gloom.* PERCY *closing the doors* R.*)*

MRS. MOSSOP. Dear Lady Caroline, it's too romantic ! Are you
certain ?

LADY CAROLINE. Well, I don't say that they'll declare themselves to-night. You know how tiresome young lovers are !

DEAN. Give them time, dear lady—a little time to overcome
their very natural diffidence. *(Moving across* L. *to fire.)*

LADY CAROLINE. Still, it would be so *satisfactory* if we could get
them to announce it to-night.

MRS. MOSSOP. Wouldn't it be too thrilling if they did, Captain
Plummer ?

PLUMMER *(pulling himself together).* If who did what ?

MRS. MOSSOP. If Maud and Reggie announced their engagement.

*(*PLUMMER *relapses into gloom again.)*

LADY CAROLINE. Why, there is Reggie !

*(*REGGIE *has appeared at the windows in a most excited condition.
He is waving his cutting from " Weekly Heartsease.")*

Reggie darling !

REGGIE. What ho, Mum ! What ho—and again what ho !
One thousand whats and one million hoes !

LADY CAROLINE *(eagerly).* Have you anything to tell mother,
dear ?

REGGIE. Have I anything to tell mother ? Have I anything
to tell the League of Nations ? I'm engaged. I've done it ! I've
pulled it off ! I've got her !

LADY CAROLINE *(throwing her arms round his neck).* My boy !
(Turning to the others.) Reggie has some news for you all—a glorious
surprise.

MRS. MOSSOP. Oh, Reggie, I am so glad.

DEAN. Congratulations, Reggie !

REGGIE. And all done on lemonade, Dean !

(*All shake hands with him, including* PLUMMER, *who does so in a most heroic fashion.*)

PERCY (*to* LADY CAROLINE). That puts the lid on the man from Switzerland—what ?

LADY CAROLINE. Yes, thank Heaven ! But where is she, Reggie ? I shan't be happy until I've given her a real hug. Where are you hiding her, you selfish boy ?

REGGIE. That's all right, Mum. She's waiting round the corner, as good as gold. I'll fetch her. Don't go away, anybody ! (*Incoherently.*) Oh, blessed Albertina ! (*He goes out by the windows and to* L.)

(ALBERTINA *appears at the top of the stairs, evidently attracted by the hubbub and the sound of her name.* REGGIE *reappears immediately with* MISS FARADAY *on his arm.*)

Here she is ! She's going to marry me ! She's told me so ! Alice !

(*There is an astonished silence.* KEGGS *appears* R.)

ALBERTINA (*whispering down the stairs to him*). He's got the wrong one !

(KEGGS *smiles triumphantly.*)

LADY CAROLINE (*finding her voice at last*). Miss Faraday ?

REGGIE. Alice to you, Mum, from now on. (*To* MISS FARADAY.) Darling, she wants to give you a real hug. Go to it. (*Pushing* MISS FARADAY *towards* LADY CAROLINE.)

ALICE (*dramatically*). Mother ! ! !

LADY CAROLINE (*recoiling*). But, my dear boy, what does this mean ?

REGGIE. It means that dear little Alice has accepted me. Haven't you, darling ?

MISS FARADAY. Yes, darling, I have.

REGGIE. Can you believe it ?

LADY CAROLINE (*grimly*). I can.

REGGIE. And she's going to marry me, aren't you, darling ?

MISS FARADAY. Yes, darling, I am.

REGGIE. Can you believe that ?

LADY CAROLINE. No !

REGGIE (*bewildered*). Why not ?

LADY CAROLINE. Because I forbid it.

REGGIE. But you said——

LADY CAROLINE. Never mind what I said. I am your mother and I forbid it.

(MISS FARADAY *nudges* REGGIE *and whispers. He nods back.*)

REGGIE.   In that case, Mum, I'm very sorry, but I'm a lot over twenty-one, and you have no say in the matter at all. Alice reminded me of that.   Dear little Alice! (*Putting his arm round her, they smile at one another affectionately.*)

PERCY.   But where the devil's Maud?

REGGIE.   Maud?   I don't know.   Is she missing?   I know— perhaps she's done a guy with the poet.

LADY CAROLINE (*in a horrified voice*).   Is *he* here—again?

REGGIE.   I expect so.   You can't keep a fellow like that out of anywhere.   (*Recollecting.*)   Why, of course he's here!   He was the man disguised as a jug of claret cup, wasn't he, Keggs?

KEGGS (*woodenly*).   I fail to comprehend, sir.

LADY CAROLINE (*desperately*).   Reggie, listen to me!   You say this man has got into the house again?

REGGIE.   Yes.

(*Two figures in men's overcoats and hats are seen stealing past the windows.*)

LADY CAROLINE.   Then where is he?

REGGIE (*idiotically*).   I don't know.   Does it matter?   (*Squeezing Miss Faraday again.*)

ALBERTINA (*suddenly, pointing from the stairs out of the window*). There he is—and 'er with him!   Stop them!

(*All turn and look, first at* ALBERTINA, *then out of the windows.* PERCY *is the first to move.*)

PERCY.   Hey, there—stop!

(*He dashes out of the window and seizes the smaller figure, which struggles.   It is* LADY MAUD.   PERCY *drags her into the room. She pulls off her felt hat, and stares defiantly about her.*)

(*Music starts.   "Fox Trot" pp till Curtain.*)

LADY CAROLINE.   Maud!

(GEORGE *has followed* LADY MAUD *and* PERCY.   *He now puts his hand on* PERCY'S *shoulder and removes him from* LADY MAUD. *All the guests present withdraw tactfully, going out* L.   *The family are left alone.*   KEGGS *is at the door* R., ALBERTINA *at foot of stairs.*)

GEORGE.   Now then, Percy, go easy with your sister.   Remember what happened last time?

PERCY.   I do remember what happened last time!   Perhaps you don't.   You had to jump over those battlements.   And you're going to do it again, in about two ticks; and this time——

GEORGE.   Oh, shut up!

(PERCY *goes back to* LADY PRUDENCE.)

LADY CAROLINE. Maud, what does this mean ?

(LADY MAUD *looks up at* GEORGE, *who comes to her assistance.*)

GEORGE (*calmly*). Lady Maud is coming to London with me.
PERCY. Oh, is she ? What for ?

(GEORGE *is silent.*)

REGGIE. Don't ask silly questions, Percy. They're going to
get married—like Alice and me. (*Suddenly.*) I say, I've got an
idea ! Let's all go up together now and make a mixed foursome
of it ? Are you on ?
LADY MAUD.
MISS FARADAY. }Yes !
GEORGE.

REGGIE. Then fall in ! Good-bye, everybody ! Good-bye,
Mum. I should love to kiss you, but you might bite me. Come on,
Alice ! (*Going to the door* L.)
LADY CAROLINE (*desperately*). Stop them, Percy ! (*Remaining*
C.)
PERCY. How the devil can I ?

(*All four are at the door* L. *now.* REGGIE *throws it open.* LORD
MARSHMORETON *appears on the stairs, in hat and coat, carrying a
small suit-case. No one sees him but* ALBERTINA, *who makes way
for him, awestruck.*)

LADY CAROLINE. Maud, stop ! You are under twenty-one. I
forbid this !
REGGIE. You can't, Mum. It's not your job.
LADY CAROLINE. Then her father shall forbid it.
LORD MARSHMORETON (*from the staircase, loudly*). Her father
won't do anything so damn silly !

(*All start and turn to* R.)

Her father knows a good man when he sees one. If Maud wants
to marry this young fellow, she shall have him. (*Crossing to* L.C.)
Take her, my boy, and good luck to you both.
LADY CAROLINE. But, Harry, we know nothing about this man.
LORD MARSHMORETON (*turning to her*). I know more than you
think. I've been making inquiries. He's all right.
LADY CAROLINE. Where did you make inquiries ?
LORD MARSHMORETON. Never you mind ! (*Turning to* REGGIE.)
Reggie, what are you doing with your arm round that girl's neck ?
REGGIE. I rather thought of marrying her, Uncle Harry.
LORD MARSHMORETON. No ! Really ? You mean it ?
REGGIE. Of course I mean it. And so does she !
LORD MARSHMORETON (*piously*). Heaven be praised ! Right
away ?

E

REGGIE. To-morrow morning. Before the dear old Registrar of St. George's.

LORD MARSHMORETON. Let me give you a lift. My car's at the door. I'm off to London myself, for a holiday. I'm fed up with this whole damn household. Are you coming?

REGGIE. } Rather!
ALICE.

LORD MARSHMORETON (*taking* LADY MAUD's *arm*). You too, Maud! (*To* GEORGE.) And you too! Let's be off! Good night, Caroline!

GEORGE (*interposing*). Lord Marshmoreton, I can't go on false pretences. I must explain——

LORD MARSHMORETON. George Bevan——

(KEGGS *and* ALBERTINA *start.*)

do you want to marry my daughter or do you not?

GEORGE (*simply*). I'd give anything in the world to marry your daughter, sir.

LORD MARSHMORETON. Then what are you standing there for? Come on!

LADY CAROLINE (*desperately*). Harry, why not wait till the morning, at least.

LORD MARSHMORETON. Why? Because my bedroom has been turned into a ladies' cloakroom! If you imagine I'm going to lie in bed, watching skinny-legged young women tighten their suspenders under my very nose, you're all damn well mistaken!

(*Exits first with* LADY MAUD. REGGIE *and* MISS FARADAY *follow.* GEORGE *goes last.*)

CURTAIN.

(PICTURE :—LADY CAROLINE *faints on to settee* R.C. PERCY *fans her with handkerchief.* KEGGS *brings drink from table up* R.C. LADY PRUDENCE *waves to the others, at the door* L.)

To face page 67]

ACT III

The SCENE *is a corner of Ye Dolly Varden Tea Shoppe, Hanover Square. It is decorated in pseudo-rustic style, with white plaster, black beams, and chintz curtains. There are antique black-letter notices hanging on the walls, advertising " Ye Olde-Worlde Strawberry Sundae, 2s.," etc.*

The main door is R. *A large window up* R.O. *A counter* L.O. *up stage. A swing door is down* L. (*opening on and off*). *Three tables are seen with plenty of chairs.*

(*When the* CURTAIN *rises,* MISS MOULD, *one of the attendants, is laying out cakes on the counter. She is an unromantic young woman in spectacles, wearing the costume of a stage milkmaid of last century— flounced chintz skirt, mob-cap, etc. She makes no attempt at any time to live up to her Arcadian surroundings.*)

(KEGGS, *wearing a black tail-coat and bowler hat, enters from the street door* R.)

KEGGS. Good morning, Miss. Nice morning.

MISS MOULD. Is it ? I haven't noticed. (*Pointing.*) You'd better take that table. (*Mechanically.*) Coffee ? Chocolate ? Strawberry ice ?

KEGGS. Nothing of that kind, I thank you. The fact is, Miss, I was wondering if you could do me a special favour.

MISS MOULD. Oh! (*Morosely.*) We aren't licensed here, you know. (*Moving to* R. *slightly.*)

KEGGS. You mistake me, Miss. I merely took the liberty of popping in to inquire if you could inform me as to the whereabouts of the St. George's Registrar's Office.

MISS MOULD. Oh, is that all ? Lots of 'em do that. (*Crossing him to the door and pointing.*) There you are, just opposite.

KEGGS. Thank you. (*Moving to* R.)

MISS MOULD. Going to be married ?

KEGGS. Me ? No dam fea——! (*Smiling.*) Such was 'ardly my intention, Miss !

MISS MOULD. Oh! Well, I was just going to say that if you were, we could do the wedding-breakfast for you. Lots of couples drop in here when it's all over. They seem to need something, quick. (*Moving to behind the counter up* L.C.)

KEGGS. Oh, they come here, do they ? That's interesting.

MISS MOULD (*suddenly*). Well, if that isn't the rotten limit ! (*She brings out a tray of used cups and saucers from under the counter.*) That's Ada, that is !

KEGGS. Ada, Miss ?

MISS MOULD. Yes. We're all ladies in this place, you see ; so we keep a strong young girl to do the washing-up. And that's how she does it ! Shoves last night's cups and saucers under the counter and goes to the pictures ! And now, at eleven o'clock in the morning, she hasn't even showed her face ! That's what comes of trying to educate them up to our level !

KEGGS. Very true, Miss. I 'ave precisely similar trouble with my own lower domestics.

MISS MOULD (*crossing from behind the counter to* C. *and moving towards the swing door* L. *with the tray*). Well, I suppose I must do these myself. It's my turn for morning duty ; the other young ladies don't come till one. So long !

KEGGS. Good day, Miss.

(MISS MOULD *goes out* L. *through swing door.*)

(KEGGS *turns and goes towards the door* R.)

(ALBERTINA *enters from the street door* R. *in her Sunday dress and hat. They meet, face to face.*)

Young blighted Albertina !

ALBERTINA. 'Ullo, Uncle Albert ! (*Crossing in front of him to* C.)

KEGGS. How did you get here ?

ALBERTINA. I changed my frock the moment the guests was gone, and 'opped into the milk-train. How did you get here ?

KEGGS (*loftily*). I motored up, of course, in the Rolls, with her ladyship and Master Percy. And may I ask what you've come to London for ?

ALBERTINA. As usual, to protect the interests of my client.

KEGGS. And may I inquire who your client is, now you've lost Reggie ?

ALBERTINA. Mr. George Bevan, late of The Field, now at the top of the betting ! You slipped up there, Keggs ! What price your poet from Switzerland this morning ?

KEGGS. You poor deluded female !

ALBERTINA. What do you mean ?

KEGGS. George Bevan's no good to you. He isn't the poet at all. He's just a blind—a red herring. I've got the real tip straight from Maud's mouth.

ALBERTINA. Who is it, then ? What's his name ?

KEGGS. That's my business. Anyhow, George's number is up.
ALBERTINA. What do you mean ?
KEGGS. He's going to be arrested.
ALBERTINA. What for ? (*Sinking on to chair* R. *of the table* L.C.)
KEGGS. Lots of things ! Pinching Mr. Reggie's second-best
dress-suit ! 'E's come up to town in it—with a dozen spoons and
forks in the tail-pockets, for all we know. (*Proudly.*) I thought
of that.
ALBERTINA (*horrified*). But 'e's a gentleman ! (*Rises.*)
KEGGS. 'E's a crook, with no visible means of subsistence !
And he's a suspected person found on enclosed premises with felon-
ious intent ! And I rather fancy you're for it as an accessory.
ALBERTINA. Me ?
KEGGS (*forcing* ALBERTINA *back down on to the chair*). Yes. I'm
sorry, my girl, but you shouldn't try to pit your brains against
mine. Well, I can't stop here bandying words with you : I must
fetch Percy and Aunt Caroline.

(ALBERTINA *rises*.)

So long ! You can tear up that ticket ! (*Going out triumphantly
door* R.)

(ALBERTINA *sinks down again in the chair at* R. *of table and gazes
after* KEGGS, *calling him names in dumb-show*.)

(*Enter* L. MISS MOULD, *with a tray of cakes, which she places on counter
up* L.C.)

MISS MOULD (*coming down* R.). What can I get you ?
ALBERTINA. I could do with a cup of tea and a bite of bread-
and-butter. I've 'ad no breakfast, and I shall need something
before the morning's out.
MISS MOULD (*after surveying her*). That'll be two-and-six.
ALBERTINA. Two-and-six ?
MISS MOULD. Yes. We only do high-class trade here.
ALBERTINA. But I've only got fourpence. I spent the rest of
my money on a railway-ticket.
MISS MOULD. Oh ! Come to get married ? Eloping ?
ALBERTINA. No. I'm a sort of bridesmaid. (*Wistfully.*) I
suppose you 'aven't got a stale bun left over from yesterday ?
MISS MOULD. We've got lots, but we shall be using them. (*Sud-
denly.*) I'll tell you what. Have you ever done any washing-up ?
ALBERTINA. Washing-up ? (*Carelessly.*) Oh, now and then,
when the servants are out.
MISS MOULD. Then go and wash up the cups and saucers in
there, and you can make yourself some tea over the gas-ring while
you're doing it. Will you ?
ALBERTINA. Like a bird, I will ! (*Rising and moving to swing
door* L.)

MISS MOULD. You're sure you know how ?

ALBERTINA (*at door*). I'll manage somehow.

(*Exits by the swing door down* L.)

(MISS MOULD *goes to the window behind the counter and begins to put out the cakes.*)

(*There is a distant sound of singing outside*—REGGIE'S *voice. He passes the window, and enters, in immaculate wedding costume.*)

REGGIE (*singing*). Ding-dong, ding-dong, ding-dong, my steed fly on !

For it is my wedding morning !

And the bride so gay in—tumtiddy-ay,

For the day is now herself ador-or-or-or-or-orning !

Ding-dong, ding-dong, ding-dong, ding-dong, tum-tiddy-um-tum !

(REGGIE *enters here, on a top note, and raps on the table, calling* "Dolly !" MISS MOULD *comes down, and glares at him over her spectacles. He takes off his hat with a sweeping gesture.*)

A fair and blithe good morning to you, Miss Varden ! You are Miss Varden herself, I suppose ?

MISS MOULD. No : it's a trade name. I'm one of the lady assistants here.

REGGIE. I see. I wonder if you would mind telling me your real name ? I should like to know you better.

MISS MOULD. My name's Miss Mould.

REGGIE. Miss Mould ! Delightful ! Leafy ! Spring-like ! Like the day ! Look at it. Sunny ! Breezy ! Balmy ! Balmy— that's the word. (*Handing her his hat.*)

MISS MOULD. You're right there. (*Putting his hat on the table in the window up* R.) Can I do anything for you ?

REGGIE. Yes.

MISS MOULD. Coffee—choc——?

REGGIE. Can you tell me the second verse of The Yeoman's Wedding Song ? It has slipped my memory for the moment.

MISS MOULD. I can't oblige you.

REGGIE. Never mind ; I shall get it presently. (*Humming.*) Tum-tum-tum-tum tumty iddity-um——

MISS MOULD. You've come along to get married, I suppose ?

REGGIE. Yes ; how did you guess ?

MISS MOULD. Where's the other one ?

REGGIE. Little Alice ? She's getting a frock, and fixing her face. She'll be along presently, bless her ! Give her time. You know what women are !

MISS MOULD (*sarcastically*). Oh no, we never see one. We live opposite to a Registrar's !

REGGIE (*raptly*). The Registrar's ! (*Going up to window.*) Just

look at it ! Romance in every stone ! What is the Registrar like ?
A dear old chap, I suppose, with white whiskers, and a frilled shirt.
Do you know him ? Do you know his people ?

Miss Mould. I've never seen him.

Reggie. No: I didn't think you had. Never mind ! Does
he cater for mixed foursomes at all, do you know ?

Miss Mould (R.C.). Marry two couples at once, do you mean ?

Reggie. Yes. Little Alice and myself, and Maud and——

Miss Mould. You don't seem quite sure who you're going to
marry. You'd better take a chair and sit quiet a bit. (*Moving
up.*)

Reggie (*sitting L. of table L.C.*). What a splendid idea ! I will !
(*Sits humming.*) Tum-tum-tum—I say, Miss Mould.

Miss Mould (*up at window, laying out cakes*). What ?

Reggie. Don't worry about that second verse : I've remem-
bered it. (*Rising and singing. Going up to the counter L.C.*)

The sun is high, is high in the morning sky,
And the church will soon be filling.
We must not wait, we must not wait—
For were we late, they'd deem the groom
Unwil-hi-hi-hi-hi-hi-hilling !

    Ding-dong——

(*Enter from R., Miss Faraday, in a smart new frock and hat. Reggie
is now leaning over the counter singing to Miss Mould, with his
back to the door.*)

Miss Faraday (*sharply*). Reggie !

Reggie (*turning and hurrying down to her*). Darling !

Miss Faraday. What are you whispering to that girl for ?

Reggie. I was singing to her about you, sweetheart.

Miss Faraday. And now I suppose you've come to sing to me
about her.

(*Miss Faraday looks doubtfully towards Miss Mould, who still
has her back turned.*)

Reggie. Oh, *that's* all right, dear. Walk round and take a look
at her from the front !

(*Miss Faraday walks up to L. and has a look at Miss Mould's face,
and then comes down with a forgiving smile.*)

How wonderful you look !

Miss Faraday (*preening herself*). Do you like me ?

Reggie (*ecstatically*). Do I like you ? (*Galloping hobby-horse-
wise down R.*)

And the bride, so gay in tum-tiddy aye
For the fray—day !—is now herself——

MISS FARADAY (*silencing him*). Reggie, where have you been since breakfast ?

REGGIE. Word of honour, dear—nowhere, except my tailor's.

MISS FARADAY (*suspiciously*). Sure ?

REGGIE. Certain. The other places don't open until eleven-thirty, anyhow. Where's Maud ?

MISS FARADAY (*sitting at table* L.). I left her at the Berkeley, getting ready. She seemed to have something on her mind, poor thing. Do you know, Reggie, once or twice I thought she was going to cry.

REGGIE (*coming to table and sitting* R. *of her*). Just a little nervous at facing the starting-gate for the first time. Are you feeling all right, precious ?

MISS FARADAY (*calmly*). Quite all right, thank you.

REGGIE. Not frightened, or anything ?

MISS FARADAY. Why should I be, dear ?

REGGIE. How do you know I won't turn out a fearful tyrant and bully, and what not ?

MISS FARADAY (*smiling*). How do you know *I* won't ?

REGGIE. You ? My little, shrinking, timid angel ! Don't be silly !

(*Enter* LADY MAUD *and* GEORGE *from door* R. GEORGE *is wearing an ordinary lounge-suit.*)

GEORGE. Ahem !

REGGIE. Ah, here comes the bride—the other one !

LADY MAUD (*who is looking rather subdued*). Hallo, Reggie ! You are a swell ! (*To* MISS FARADAY.) I love your frock, Alice.

MISS FARADAY (*smiling and rising*). Thank you, Lady Maud.

REGGIE (*to* GEORGE). I adore your wedding trousers, George.

GEORGE. They're not my wedding trousers. I'm not going to be married.

REGGIE. Maud, old thing, what is our friend burbling about ?

LADY MAUD (*sitting* L. *of table*). It's all going to be rather difficult to explain, Reggie.

REGGIE. Then I'll have a cup of coffee, to clear my intellect. Miss Mould !

(MISS MOULD *comes down.*)

That is Miss Mould. (*Business of introduction.*) Maud, little Alice, and dear old——

MISS MOULD (*quite unmoved by all this ceremony*). Coffee ? Chocolate ? Strawberry ice ?

REGGIE (*imitating her*). Strawberry aice ?

LADY MAUD. Coffee, Miss Mould. For four.

MISS MOULD. Righto ! (*Goes out by the door* L.)

REGGIE. George, old thing, go and roll yourself up in a chocolate éclair for a moment. (GEORGE *goes up to window*.) Now, Maud, what does he mean?

LADY MAUD. He means that I'm going to marry somebody else—Austen Gray.

REGGIE. Austen Gray. Who's he?

LADY MAUD. The man from Switzerland—the real man from Switzerland. Mr. Bevan is just a friend—a real friend.

REGGIE (*much confused. To* GEORGE). You aren't a poet after all?

GEORGE (*coming down* R.). No; it was a case of mistaken identity. I'm only a humble musician.

REGGIE. Oh—musician? (*Thinking*.) Musician—George Bevan. (*Rising*.) *The* George Bevan? The man who wrote The Banana Girl?

GEORGE. Guilty.

REGGIE. That settles everything. Maud, you've *got* to marry him. Do you realize who he is?

LADY MAUD. Yes, I do. But——

REGGIE. Well, you simply can't throw away the chance of a lifetime like this—the chance of a bunch of centuries! The first distinction that has happened to our family since Hengist and Horsa came and stayed with us for a long week-end!

(MISS MOULD *enters with coffee on a tray which she places on the table* L.C.)

MISS MOULD. Coffee. (*She goes up to the counter again*.)

LADY MAUD (*beginning to pour out the coffee*). I'm sorry, Reggie!

MISS FARADAY (*to* LADY MAUD). Does Lord Marshmoreton know, Lady Maud?

LADY MAUD. No. I tried to explain to him at breakfast, but he was so grumpy and absent-minded that I couldn't.

MISS FARADAY. Is he coming to our wedding?

LADY MAUD. No; he has an appointment somewhere at half-past eleven. (*Restlessly*.) It's after eleven now. (*Looking at watch*.) I wonder where Austen is. I was to meet him here. (*Rising and going* R. *to the door*.)

REGGIE. Well, perhaps he won't turn up. We'll hope for the best, anyhow. (*Putting lumps of sugar into cup*.)

MISS MOULD. Perhaps you'd like a few buns? (*Putting plate on the table*.) Are you the four that want to get married all together?

REGGIE. Practically.

MISS MOULD. What do you mean, practically?

REGGIE. We could go ahead and do it now, but this gentleman—(*indicating* GEORGE)—is only an understudy. Our star is a trifle late. They usually are.

MISS MOULD. You'll get married in separate pairs, if you'll take my advice.

REGGIE. Why ?

MISS MOULD. The wrong one might get you. (*Exits by door* L.)

REGGIE (*standing*). Did you 'ear what I 'eard ? (*Sitting again.*)

LADY MAUD. I think she's right, Reggie. You and Alice had better run along, or you'll miss your turn. George will keep me company. Won't you, George ?

GEORGE. Of course I will. Go to it, Reggie !

REGGIE (*rising*). Shall we, darling ? (*Moving up and getting hat from table up* R., *and coming down again.*)

MISS FARADAY (*smiling*). Whatever you say, dear. (*Taking his arm.*)

REGGIE. I'll say we will—and split a chocolate sundae jointly before facing the big world together.

LADY MAUD. Where are you going for your honeymoon ?

REGGIE. Abroad. And I fancy we shall stay there until Time, the Great Healer, has ironed out a few creases in the family circle at home. (*Moving up towards the door* R.)

MISS FARADAY (*at the door*). I'm taking Reggie on a tour of the Cathedral cities of Europe, Lady Maud.

REGGIE. Won't that be fun ? There *is* a cathedral in Paris, isn't there, darling ?

MISS FARADAY. Yes, dear.

REGGIE. And at Monte Carlo ?

MISS FARADAY (*firmly*). No, dear.

REGGIE. Right, darling. We'll build one.

(*They go out together by the door* R.)

(LADY MAUD, *who has followed them to the door, waves till they are out of sight, then turns and walks restlessly about.* GEORGE *is sitting at the table.*)

GEORGE (*brightly*). Feeling excited ?

LADY MAUD (*in a subdued voice*). Not exactly excited.

GEORGE. Just a pleasant thrill—eh ? I expect he's feeling excited all right. I know I should.

LADY MAUD (*turning and looking at him*). Would you ?

GEORGE. *Would* I ? If I were walking down that street, knowing that you were sitting here waiting for me—watching that door, to see me come through it—would I be excited ? I'd be delirious ! (*Rising.*) And I wouldn't be walking, either ; I'd be breaking the quarter mile record ! (*Crossing up.*) Excited ? Ooh !

(LADY MAUD, *looking after him, sits at* R. *of the table. He turns and recovers himself.*)

However, that's not on the agenda, is it ? (*Sitting opposite to her.*) Tell me some more about him. How did you first meet him ? Where did you first meet him ? In a crowd ? All alone ? Or what ? It must be a wonderful memory.

LADY MAUD.   I met him at Mürren, on a hillside, in a mist.
He'd been up on a mountain-top all day, by himself—for inspiration,
I suppose.

GEORGE (*determined to be interested*).   I see.   One of your rare
solitary spirits.   And he was thin and pale, and very delicate.

LADY MAUD.   Yes.   He wasn't a bit imposing.   His clothes were
all wrong, too.

GEORGE.   It sounds like a case of pity at first sight.

LADY MAUD.   I suppose it was, really.   For the first few days
after I met him I felt more like his mother than anything else.   He
was so unpractical—so helpless——

GEORGE.   No eye to the main chance ?

LADY MAUD.   No ; he didn't seem to be able to look after himself.

GEORGE.   So you promised to do it for him ?

LADY MAUD.   Yes.   He lived too much in a world of his own ;
and there are some rather jolly things to do in this world, aren't
there ?

GEORGE.   Rather !   Especially when you do them in the right
company.

LADY MAUD.   Yes—rather.

(*Their eyes meet for a moment.*)

It'll be pretty awful if I can't drag him down to my level, won't
it ? (*She smiles.*)

GEORGE.   Don't you worry about that, Maud.   There's no level
higher than yours. (*Rising.*)   Well, I must be off.   If you don't
mind, I won't meet him in your presence.   You understand ?

(LADY MAUD *nods.*)

I must get back to the old homestead, and rewrite two musical
numbers that have fallen down on us.

(LADY MAUD *rises too.*)

LADY MAUD (*standing* L. *of table*).   I'm glad you've got your work
to do. (*Giving him her hand.*)   Good-bye.   You've been rather
wonderful to me.   I wish I could—oh, it's no use saying anything !

GEORGE.   Well, I've known you, anyhow.   Now, you sit down
there—(*putting her* L. *of table*)—

(*She obeys reluctantly.*)

—and face this door, and imagine it's a cloud of mist on a Swiss
hillside ; and keep on watching till you see him !   Good-bye !

(*Exits by the door* R.)

(MISS MOULD *enters from* L.)

MISS MOULD.   Have you finished, Miss ?

LADY MAUD.   Not quite. (*Beginning to drink her coffee.*)

MISS MOULD. Have the other couple gone across?
LADY MAUD. Yes.
MISS MOULD. That half-witted lad will be singing a different tune when he comes back. She's going to be the big noise in that family.
LADY MAUD (*smiling*). Is she?
MISS MOULD. Yes. I see a lot of 'em here, and I usually know. Your young gentleman's a bit late, isn't he?
LADY MAUD. I expect he'll be here presently.

(AUSTEN GRAY *appears, passing the window up* R.)

MISS MOULD. Titivating, I expect. You stay where you are. You'll have the place to yourselves at this time of the morning. (*Goes up to the window.*)

(*Enter* AUSTEN GRAY *from door* R. *He is rather plump, very correctly dressed, and utterly conventional—a complete surprise in every way.* LADY MAUD *suddenly sees him. For a moment she does not recognize him; then she gasps with astonishment.*)

LADY MAUD. Austen! (*Rising, and speaking, facing to front.*) The cloud of mist! (*Sitting again* L. *of table.*)
GRAY. Good morning, Maud! Here you are! (*Taking off hat and gloves, rather unconcernedly, placing them on chair above table.*) I'm sorry to be late: I thought a little exercise would do me good, so I walked.

(LADY MAUD *still continues to stare at him. He snaps his fingers to attract* MISS MOULD.)

(*Sitting on* R. *of the table.*) Here, Miss! Ps't, ps't!

(MISS MOULD *comes down and brings the menu.*)

Hot chocolate, please, with plenty of whipped cream. And see that it *is* hot! Take away those buns, and bring something eatable. Chocolate éclairs, or cream puffs! And hurry, please!

(MISS MOULD *looks at him witheringly, and moves away.*)

And, Miss! Ps't, ps't! (*Snapping his fingers again.*) Bring some hot tea-cakes, with plenty of butter on them.

(MISS MOULD *takes down the order and goes out* L.)

Well, that's that! Maud, you haven't changed a bit.
LADY MAUD. Haven't I?
GRAY. No: you're just the same. I think I have put on a little weight. I don't know if you notice it?
LADY MAUD. It's just perceptible, Austen.
GRAY (*sitting*). After all, as Mrs. Abner Smith said, I owed myself a couple of stone.

LADY MAUD. Mrs. Abner Smith? Who is she?

GRAY. A widow. The poor lady has been twice a widow. I've been spending six months on her yacht—the West Indies and Florida; in fact, I have been acting as her private secretary. A most cultured woman, most cultured—from Pittsburgh. She had a Japanese cook—a perfect treasure. By the way, have you ever eaten a marvellous fish called the pompano—from the coast of Florida?

LADY MAUD. I don't think so.

GRAY. Well, if you do, be careful to have it broiled, not fried. Otherwise you lose the flavour. Tell the waiter you *must* have it broiled, with plenty of melted butter, and a little parsley, and plain boiled potatoes.

LADY MAUD. Yes, Austen.

(MISS MOULD *re-enters with chocolate, etc.*)

MISS MOULD. Chocolate—whipped cream—cream puffs—buttered tea-cakes.

GRAY (*taking the cover off the tea-cakes and gazing at them indignantly*). I thought so! I expected as much! I particularly asked for plenty of butter on these. For Heaven's sake bring me the butter-dish, and I'll do it myself!

(MISS MOULD *crosses up to counter, after giving him another glare.*)

They simply don't understand a meal like this at these places. You have to go to the country to get the real thing. On our homeward trip we called in at Plymouth, and I took Mrs. Abner Smith to tea in a real Devonshire farm-house. Home-made cakes and jam of every kind, and real clotted Devonshire cream.

(MISS MOULD *places the butter-dish before him and goes out* L.)

Ah, that's better. (*Spreading butter on the buns and beginning a hearty meal.*) By the way, would you care for anything, Maud?

LADY MAUD. No, thank you, I've had a cup of coffee.

GRAY. Very bad for you, very bad indeed, without something solid to absorb it. Never drink without eating. (*Finishes his cup of chocolate.*) Did you come up from Totleigh this morning?

LADY MAUD. Yes—quite early.

GRAY. Oh! (*Coldly.*) I was in two minds about keeping this appointment, Maud.

LADY MAUD. Why, Austen?

GRAY. I think you might have warned me. You have wounded me, Maud—deeply. (*Eating a cream puff in one mouthful.*)

LADY MAUD. What do you mean?

GRAY (*shaking his head sadly*). Could you not have waited?

LADY MAUD. Waited? I have been here for nearly half an hour.

GRAY. I was not referring to that.

LADY MAUD. Then what are you referring to ?

GRAY. I am referring to Mr. George Bevan !

(LADY MAUD *stares at him in astonishment.*)

I hope you will be very happy with him, Maud. I am not angry with you—oh, no ! What right had I to expect that you would be proof against a separation of twelve months ? None ! It was my own fault, for trusting too implicitly in a young, shallow girl. All last winter you were my constant thought—(*eating another whole cream puff*)—and I—(*with a sad little laugh*)—foolishly dreamed that I was yours. But already I was forgotten. (*Sadly.*) Mr. George Bevan. (*Eating another cream puff, and gazing at her solemnly.*)

LADY MAUD. Austen, what on earth are you talking about ?

GRAY (*in a slightly muffled voice*). This ! (*Producing a copy of the "Morning Post," and laying it before her.*) Read that, Maud !

LADY MAUD (*reading*). "A marriage has been arranged, and will take place in July, between Lady Maud Veronica Moreton Marsh, only daughter of the Earl of Marshmoreton, and Mr. George Bevan." Who on earth put this in ?

GRAY. That is not for me to say. But it would have been kinder to have forewarned me.

LADY MAUD. But, Austen, I simply don't understand——

GRAY. Are you engaged to this man, or are you not, Maud ? Answer me that !

LADY MAUD. Why, of course I'm n—— (*Checking herself, and turning square to the audience.*) I shan't tell you !

GRAY. As I thought ! Mrs. Abner Smith was right. I said she was wrong, but she was right. She said : "Baby—(*eating another puff*)—that girl is too young, too flighty, not sufficiently mature, to be faithful."

LADY MAUD (*indignantly*). Ooh ! How dare she talk like that ? (*Rising.*) Or you either ?

GRAY. Have you been faithful ? Have I been your only thought ? Did you pray and pray, during those months of separation, that I might be given back to you ?

LADY MAUD (*facing square to audience*). If I did, I certainly didn't expect to get back about twice as much as I prayed for !

GRAY (*rising*). Maud, that remark is in execrable taste. I see I have had a fortunate escape. (*Moving up to door R.*) Good morning !

LADY MAUD (*incredulously*). You're really going ? For good ?

GRAY. Yes. It will be best for both of us. I shall never see you again.

LADY MAUD. I expect Mrs. Abner Smith will see to that, dear !

GRAY. I have done with schoolgirls—for ever !

(*Exit* AUSTEN GRAY, *indignantly, by the door* R.)

(LADY MAUD *dances round the shop, then picks up the " Morning Post " and reads the notice again.*)

LADY MAUD. "A marriage has been arranged"—Oh, bless you, whoever put it in! (*Kisses the paper.*) Bless you! Oh, George, George, where are you? (*Crossing up to the door* R.)

(*Enter* ALBERTINA, *wiping her mouth, from the door* L.)

ALBERTINA (*over her shoulder*). Thank you kindly, Miss Mould. I've dried them as well. (*Turning and seeing* LADY MAUD.) My lady!

LADY MAUD (*recognizing her*). Albertina? Is it you?

ALBERTINA. Yes, my lady—Albertina, the between-maid. 'Ave you seen Mr. X—Mr. Bevan.

LADY MAUD. Yes, but he's gone.

ALBERTINA. You mustn't let him go, my lady. He's in danger. They're trying to pinch him!

LADY MAUD. Who?

ALBERTINA. Mr. Keggs, and Percy, and that lot. We must find him and warn him. He *is* the one you truly love, my lady, isn't he?

LADY MAUD (*raptly*). He is, he is!

ALBERTINA. I knew old Keggs was swinging the lead! I knew Mr. Bevan wasn't a red 'erring. But let me help, my lady! I'm in this! I'm interested!

LADY MAUD (*divided between laughter and tears*). I know. The sweepstake! I heard about it. You shall win it, Albertina. But he's gone, and I don't know where he lives!

ALBERTINA. He's not gone, my lady. I saw him just now out of the pantry winder, popping into the Registry Office. I expect he was going to see Mr. Reggie and Miss Faraday through. Shall I fetch him? (*Moving towards the door* R.)

LADY MAUD. Yes! Run—quick!

ALBERTINA. All right, my lady!

(*Dashes out of the door* R.)

(*Re-enter* MISS MOULD.)

MISS MOULD. Where's your young gentleman?

LADY MAUD. He's gone.

MISS MOULD. Is he coming back? (*Beginning to clear up tea-things.*)

LADY MAUD. I hope not!

MISS MOULD (*nodding her head*). Oh, it's like that, is it?

LADY MAUD. Yes, it is.

MISS MOULD. They do weaken sometimes, at the last minute. Or was it you?

LADY MAUD (*smiling*). Perhaps it was both of us!

MISS MOULD. I dare say it was all ordained. We weren't put in

this world to enjoy ourselves. I suppose you know he hasn't paid
for all this slush he's been eating.

LADY MAUD. Never mind! I'll do that.

MISS MOULD (*cheering up slightly and making out the bill*). Righto !
It's tough on you, though. A young gentleman once did it on me,
one Whit-Monday at Hampton Court. Two teas, two boiled eggs,
and a water-cress—dirty tyke! Six and ten, please.

(LADY MAUD *hands her a note.*)

Thank you. (*Goes to door* L.) I suppose you'll have to look out for
a new job now, or else go back to your old one.

LADY MAUD. I'm certainly not going back to my old one.

MISS MOULD. Well, good luck, anyway! I'll fetch your change.

(*She goes out by the door* L.)

(*Enter* GEORGE, *hurriedly, from door* R.)

GEORGE. Maud!

LADY MAUD. George!

GEORGE. You want me? Albertina said it was urgent.

LADY MAUD. It is. Percy and Keggs are after you. But—(*leading him down* C.)—before they arrive, I just want to ask you a question or two. How do you stand about butter?

GEORGE. Butter? (*Staring at her in astonishment.*) What do
you mean?

LADY MAUD. Well, if you don't even know what butter means,
that's all right. Now, what's your weight?

GEORGE. Eleven stone ten. (*Smiling.*) But I don't understand.

LADY MAUD. What was it this time last year? (*Pointing at him.*)

GEORGE. About the same. I always weigh about the same.

LADY MAUD. Wonderful! George?

GEORGE. Yes?

LADY MAUD. This is very important. Have you ever been in
Florida?

GEORGE. Once.

LADY MAUD. Do you know a fish called the pompano?

GEORGE. Yes.

LADY MAUD. Tell me all about it.

GEORGE. How do you mean? It's just a fish. You eat it.

LADY MAUD. I know. Go into details.

GEORGE. There aren't any. You just eat it.

LADY MAUD (*half-hysterically*). Oh, George! (*Jumping with joy,
her hands on his shoulders.*) Bless you, bless you! No butter?
No parsley? No plain boiled waiter? You're sure?

GEORGE. Plain boi . . . Maud dear, please explain. (R.C.,
behind table.)

LADY MAUD (*crossing to table and taking up the* " Morning Post ").
Have you seen the " Morning Post " to-day?

GEORGE. No.

(REGGIE and MISS FARADAY *are seen passing the window, arm in arm.*)

LADY MAUD. You haven't been contributing to it, I suppose ?

GEORGE. Maud, Maud ! What are you talking about——

LADY MAUD. Well, somebody has. Here's a notice. Here are Reggie and Alice. Come round this corner, I want to tell you something. (*Running to counter, pointing to off up* L.) If you don't come, I'll sue you for breach of promise !

(*She runs off* L., *laughing.* GEORGE, *quite bewildered, dashes after her.*)

(*Enter* REGGIE *and* MISS FARADAY, *arm in arm, by the door* R.)

REGGIE (*striking an attitude*). Behold the blushing bridegroom ! Hallo, I could have sworn I saw Maud through the window just now.

MISS FARADAY. Perhaps she's gone down the street to meet Mr. Gray.

REGGIE (*looking at his watch*). That being so, and the sun being right over the yard-arm, what about stepping across to a little adjacent hostelry I wot of, and splicing the mainbrace ?

MISS FARADAY. No, dear ; that's all over now. (*Sitting at top of table.*)

REGGIE (*horrified*). What ?

MISS FARADAY. For you, in future, the sun will reach the yard-arm at seven p.m. and set at eleven sharp.

REGGIE. But, Alice—angel—I mean to say——

MISS FARADAY (*sweetly*). Order me a chocolate ice, please, darling.

(KEGGS *appears at the door* R.)

KEGGS (*over his shoulder*). Here they are, my lady ! Here they are, my lord ! I thought we should nab them here !

(*Enter* LADY CAROLINE *and* PERCY.)

(KEGGS *exits again by* R. *door.*)

REGGIE. My sainted mother !

LADY CAROLINE (*grimly*). Yes.

REGGIE. Come in, and give yourself a hearty welcome ! Have an ice ? Oh, stop me and buy one !

LADY CAROLINE. Am I too late ?

REGGIE. It depends on which of us you are chasing. Alice and I are already beyond human aid—interference. (*Fondly.*) Aren't we, wifie ?

MISS FARADAY. Yes, dear. Good morning, Mother.

(LADY CAROLINE *glares at her.*)

(*To* REGGIE.) Take me away and feed me. (*They go up to the counter.*)

F

PERCY.   Never mind that idiot Reggie !   It's Maud that matters.
Where is she ?
LADY CAROLINE.   Yes.   Where is Maud, Reggie ?

(LADY MAUD *and* GEORGE *reappear from up* L., *hand in hand.*)

LADY MAUD (L.C.).   Here I am, Aunt Caroline !
LADY CAROLINE (C.).   Maud, are you still single ?
LADY MAUD.   Yes, Aunt Caroline.
LADY CAROLINE.   Then come home at once.
LADY MAUD (*demurely*).   Yes, Aunt Caroline.   With George ?
LADY CAROLINE. }
PERCY.   } (R.C.).   Certainly not !
LADY MAUD.   But I'm engaged to him !
LADY CAROLINE.   Stuff and nonsense !
LADY MAUD.   But I know I am !   I've just seen it in the papers !
GEORGE.   Yes.   It's official !
LADY CAROLINE.   My dear child, what do you mean ?
LADY MAUD.   I mean this.

(GEORGE *politely hands* LADY CAROLINE *the " Morning Post.*")

GEORGE.   The first paragraph—(*pointing to announcement*)—that
little fellow there.
LADY CAROLINE (*after reading it, turning to* PERCY *and holding out
the paper*).   Percy, look at this !

(PERCY *snatches it, and reads it.*)

Maud, who put this in ?
LADY MAUD.   I don't know, Aunt Caroline.   I didn't.
LADY CAROLINE (*with decision*).   Your father must be told about
this, at once—so that he can have it contradicted.   Where is he ?
GEORGE.   I rather think that's him passing the window—with
something diaphanous clinging to his right arm——

(*All turn and look towards the door* R.)

(*Enter by the door* R. LORD MARSHMORETON, *in a rather old-fashioned
morning-coat, with a rose in his buttonhole.   He is arm in arm
with* BILLIE DORE, *in a smart muslin frock, carrying a bunch of
roses.   All the family gape at* LORD MARSHMORETON. *He is
quite unconscious of their presence.*)

LORD MARSHMORETON (C. *to* R.   *To* BILLIE).   Well, that didn't
take so long as I expected.   Come in here, while I get a taxi.
(*Fondly.*) Kiddo ! (*Turns and sees the others.*) God bless my
soul !
LADY CAROLINE.   Harry !
LADY MAUD.   Daddy ! (*Running across and flinging her arms
round him.*)

BILLIE. Well, if it isn't George Bevan. What do you know about that ? (*Crossing to him.*) Georgie, would you like to be the first to kiss a little bride ?

GEORGE. You bet I would ! (*Doing so.*)

(*Then he and* BILLIE *go up to* LORD MARSHMORETON *and* LADY MAUD *and* GEORGE *shakes hands with* LORD MARSHMORETON.)

GEORGE. Congratulations to you, sir !

LORD MARSHMORETON. Thank you very much. Billie, this is my daughter, Maud.

(LADY MAUD *and* BILLIE *shake hands, saying,* " How do you do " *and* " Pleased to meet you." *Meanwhile* GEORGE *and* LORD MARSH-MORETON *talk and laugh together.* PERCY *tries to edge into the group, fussily.* GEORGE *suddenly shakes hands with* PERCY *too, much to his annoyance. General chatter.*)

LADY CAROLINE (*shouting them all down at last*). Harry, before I take leave of my senses, will you kindly explain what all this means ? (*Moving up* L.C.)

LORD MARSHMORETON. Oh ! What ? Yes, certainly, certainly ! (*Crossing to* BILLIE *and presenting her.*) This is—er—was—Miss Billie Dore—the first sensible girl I've met for about twenty-five years. I married her about three minutes ago—

(*Sensation.*)

(LADY CAROLINE *crosses to* L.)

—and if any of you don't like the idea, you can lump it !

REGGIE (R.). But we do like it. She's a pippin ! May I kiss my Aunt William ? (*Going* C.)

MISS FARADAY (R.). Reggie ! (*Pointing to his place beside her.*)

REGGIE. Sorry ! (*Coming back, very cowed.*)

LADY MAUD. I'll do it, for the family, Reggie. (*Kisses* BILLIE.)

BILLIE. You sweet thing ! (*Looking round.*) Are there some more of the family ?

LADY MAUD. My aunt, Lady Caroline Higgins.

BILLIE (*smiling*). Pleased to meet you.

LADY CAROLINE (*coldly. Turning away*). How do you do ?

BILLIE. Who's that little feller over there, with the discontented expression ?

LADY MAUD. That's my brother Percy.

BILLIE. Good morning, Perce ! Would you like to kiss Momma ?

PERCY. No, thank you. (*Goes up to window* R.C.)

REGGIE. Mug !

LORD MARSHMORETON (*noticing* REGGIE *and* MISS FARADAY). Hallo, Reggie ! Are you and Miss Faraday married ?

F*

REGGIE. Yes, Uncle Harry.

LORD MARSHMORETON (*relieved*). Ha! I mean, congratulations!
Maud, are you?

LADY MAUD. Not yet, Daddy.

LORD MARSHMORETON. Good!

LADY MAUD (*alarmed*). Oh, Daddy!

LORD MARSHMORETON. I mean—are you in any special hurry?

LADY MAUD (*turning to* GEORGE). Are we, George?

GEORGE. Not special. Just ordinary, and frantic—that's all!

LORD MARSHMORETON. Can you wait till July?

GEORGE. Why July, sir?

LADY MAUD. I see; because that's what it says in the newspaper!

LADY CAROLINE. But who put it in the newspaper at all?

LORD MARSHMORETON. I did!

LADY CAROLINE. You?

LORD MARSHMORETON. Yes. I telephoned it to the office last
night.

LADY CAROLINE. When?

LORD MARSHMORETON. Directly after I'd had that argument
with you. (*To* GEORGE.) I'd heard all about you, my boy, from
Billie here, and I took a good square look at you last night when you
didn't know it. That made up my mind for me! You're a real
trier, and a sportsman! You shall marry him, Maud, in the Castle
Chapel, with the Dean to do the chit-chat, and your old Daddy to
give you away—and bridesmaids—and Bollinger——

REGGIE. And Percy as a page, in white satin trousers!

(REGGIE, MISS FARADAY *and* GEORGE *go up to counter.*)

LADY MAUD (*embracing her father*). Darling!

LADY CAROLINE (*coming to* L.C.). Harry, let me make one more
appeal to you. Are you going to allow your only daughter to marry
a starving poet?

LORD MARSHMORETON. He isn't a poet. He's a musician.

LADY CAROLINE. Well, it's the same thing. Don't quibble!
He's a fortune-hunter in any case.

PERCY. He probably plays a barrel-organ!

BILLIE (*hearing this, and stepping forward*). Harry—Maud—let
me come in on this hand. (*To* PERCY.) Listen to Momma, little
angel-face! Do you mean to say you never heard of George Bevan
—*the* George Bevan? Do you know that boy's the biggest writer
of song-hits in London, or out of it?

LADY CAROLINE. How could this man ever maintain Maud in
the position——? (*Crossing* R. *of table.*)

BILLIE. Maintain? Position? Listen, sister!

LADY CAROLINE (*turning horrified*). What!!...

BILLIE. —in law! Get this earful! Have you any idea what

that boy pulls down in royalties? Well, I guess George's little
weekly pay-cheque works out at about five thousand dollars per
week. Now, sister-in-law, can five thousand dollars a week make
a composer respectable ?

LADY CAROLINE (*smiling*). It would make a saxophone player
respectable. Now I come to look at him again, he seems positively
presentable ! (*Turning effusively to* GEORGE.) Why did you never
tell me all this before, my dear boy ? (*Moving up and shaking
hands.*)

(GEORGE *looks bewildered.*)

BILLIE. Go right ahead, Georgie. The track's clear ! Kiss
your aunt !

(GEORGE *kisses* LADY CAROLINE. *Sound of taxies outside the door.*)

LORD MARSHMORETON. Good ! Now let's all go and lunch at
Claridge's. You trot along, Caroline, take Percy away and give
him a cocktail, or an anæsthetic, or *something* !

(*He and* BILLIE *stand at the door.*)

LADY CAROLINE (*moving up to the door with* PERCY, *then turning
back*). We shall see you at lunch, George. (*Shaking her finger at*
LORD MARSHMORETON.) There, Harry, after all your bungling, I
have found the right man for dear Maud at last !

(*Exits by the door* R.)

GEORGE. Thank you, Lady Caroline. Keep me a place by you,
Percy !

PERCY. I shan't ! I suspect you of being a very noisy eater.

(PERCY *follows* LADY CAROLINE *out* R. *angrily.*)

LORD MARSHMORETON (*to* REGGIE *and* MISS FARADAY). You two
next.

(MISS FARADAY *and* REGGIE *cross to* R.)

And, Alice ! You can regard the Family History as finished.

BILLIE. Not on your life ! It's just beginning—isn't it, Mrs.
Reggie ?

MISS FARADAY (*with a smile at* REGGIE). Reggie's is !

REGGIE (*sadly*). Cocoa and cathedrals !

(MISS FARADAY *and* REGGIE *go out* R.)

LORD MARSHMORETON (*to* GEORGE *and* LADY MAUD). Now, you
two !

BILLIE. Dadda, be yourself ! Come when you're ready, children. You'll find the old folks waiting for you where the dry
Martinis grow !

(BILLIE *and* LORD MARSHMORETON *laugh and go out by the door* R.)

GEORGE (*going to* LADY MAUD). At last! (*Tries to take her in his arms.*)

LADY MAUD (*looking over her shoulder and pointing*). Careful, dear!

(*Enter* ALBERTINA.)

GEORGE. Albertina!

ALBERTINA. Mr. X!

GEORGE (*they shake hands*). The outsider who romped home!

(*At this moment* MISS MOULD *appears with* LADY MAUD'S *change.* LADY MAUD *goes up stage and tells her to keep it.*)

Who wins the sweep, Albertina?

ALBERTINA. I do, sir. (*Pulling out the ticket.*) There you are— The Field. It was a 'ard and bitter struggle, but it was well worth it!

GEORGE. What was the total amount?

ALBERTINA. Seventeen and sixpence, sir.

GEORGE. Will you accept this as added money? (*Giving her a five-pound note.*)

ALBERTINA (*gaping, quite unable to speak*). A fiver!

(KEGGS *appears at the door* R.)

KEGGS. His lordship is waiting, sir.

GEORGE. Thanks. Are you ready, Maud?

(*He goes up and takes her arm. They smile a good-bye to* MISS MOULD.)

ALBERTINA (*crossing towards door* R. *Turning to* KEGGS *and handing him the sweep ticket*). My poor feller! There's a consternation prize for you! (*Exit, with great dignity.*)

(LADY MAUD *and* GEORGE *embrace.*)

(KEGGS *is left holding the door open and staring at the ticket.*)

CURTAIN.

FURNITURE AND PROPERTY PLOT

ACT I

SCENE 1

Inside Doorkeeper's box.—Clock, pictures, key-board, letter-rack, towel, in rack, letters and telegrams. Bundle of letters for POSTMAN. Bundle of telegrams for MAC. Telephone and bell, and newspaper.
Outside box.—Call-board, notice-board. Form or bench R.

SCENE 2

Stage cloth to cover the whole stage. Drugget square C. to cover carpet square, which is laid for Act II. Strip of drugget to door L. and also to cover the heavy stair carpet on stairs.
2 brass stands to support a red rope which is stretched across the room and hooked to the walls below door up L. and the double doors down R.
The fireplace is down L. Large steel fittings to same.
2 chairs are L., one above and one below the fireplace.
A low-backed settee set at right angles (with back to the fireplace) L.C. Another settee, high cane-backed, at R.C.
Stool on R. of windows C. and on L. of same.
A table. *On this :—*a lamp, inkstand, pens and paper, etc.
Down R. below the double doors, 1 small chair.
The staircase is above these doors running up and off to R.
A suit of armour is set near stairs up R.C.
Tapestries are above the table L.C. and over the fireplace.
Over the L. door is the portrait of a gentleman and over the double doors R. the portrait of a lady.
On the battlements outside the windows C. are flowers, etc. A tub of roses for LORD MARSHMORETON is just outside.
Heavy curtains are at windows C. with pelmet to match same.
A bucket and syringe for LORD MARSHMORETON and a green apron.
Tickets of a sweepstake and lead pencil for KEGGS and ALBERTINA.
Motor-coat and goggles for REGGIE.
Polishing cloth for ALBERTINA.
Bag of golf sticks for LADY MAUD. Notices on cardboard for KEGGS.
Bunch of roses and a single rose for BILLIE and LORD MARSHMORETON.
Note for GEORGE and also a £1 note.
Ledger books and papers for LADY CAROLINE and MISS FARADAY.
White wand for KEGGS.
Flags, etc., about the walls.
Lanterns above doors R. and below, brackets about stage.

ACT II

The same with the following alterations :—
The table L. has been moved to the R. of the windows and is now set out with refreshments of all kinds, wines, champagne, brandy, whisky, syphons of soda, bottles of lemonade and soda.

The druggets have been removed, also the rope and its supports.
The stool is in front of the table.
A screen is placed on the stairs in front of the window.
Banks of flowers are above doors R., L. of windows O., and in fireplace L.
GEORGE, footman's dress and trick moustache.
Sweepstake tickets, pencil, etc., as before.
Hats, coats, etc., for MAUD and GEORGE.
The suit of armour has been moved.
Cigars, cigarettes, matches, ash-trays, etc., to L., near the door, for this Act.

ACT III

3 round tables. Counter up L.O.
Covered with bright covers of the same material.
Bright curtains to match with pelmets to windows up R.O.
4 stools, 7 chairs.
Trays with cakes, etc.
Coffee (fresh made and hot) in pot for 4 people.
Plate of buns, etc.
Cups and saucers, spoons, plates, knives and forks, etc.
Chocolate in cup.
Cream, sugar, etc., etc.
Butter in dish, knife for same.
Large tray of dirty cups and saucers under counter.
Vases of flowers about stage.
£1 note for LADY MAUD.
Change for MISS MOULD.
Sweepstake tickets for ALBERTINA and KEGGS.
Bunch of flowers (roses), for BILLIE.
Rose for LORD MARSHMORETON.
Newspaper folded for the wedding announcement.
Hot tea-cakes in dish with cover.
Chocolate éclairs and 4 cream puffs.
A duster and polishing cloth for the cups.

LIGHTING PLOT

ACT I

Scene 1

Dark ambers in floats and 1st batten.
Perches, R. and L.—(open limes), amber.
A strip outside the door L.—white.
No light outside the door R. (leading to the stage).
A glow from a lamp inside the doorkeeper's box.

Scene 2

Floats and Battens.—Dark amber, reds in here and there.
Perches, R. and L.—(open limes), bright amber.
Bright amber and white floods on backing and battlements.
Strip off at door L.

ACT II

Floats and Battens.—Bright amber, reds here and there.
Perches.—Bright amber (open limes) R. and L.
All lights bright as possible.
Green floods outside windows C. on battlements.
Amber strip on staircase.
Amber strips on outside doors L. and R.

ACT III

Floats and Battens.—Bright ambers and pinks.
Open limes, amber, from perches R. and L.
Floods off below door R. and outside window up R.C.—white and pink.
Dark amber strip off at swing door.
Amber (bright) strip up L. of counter.

www.ingramcontent.com/pod-product-compliance
Lightning Source LLC
LaVergne TN
LVHW051752080426
835511LV00018B/3306